Arabic

Maccabees

SCRIPTURAL RESEARCH INSTITUTE
Published by Digital Ink Productions, 2024

Copyright

Arabic Maccabees

First edition. January 3, 2024

Copyright © 2024 Scriptural Research Institute.

ISBN: 978-1-998288-66-3

Arabic Maccabees was likely composed in Palestinian Aramaic shortly after 525 AD and later translated into Arabic before the year 1200. This English translation was created by the Scriptural Research Institute in 2023.

The image used for the cover is an artistic reinterpretation of 'Mattathias refuses to sacrifice to idols' by Gustave Popelin, painted in 1882. The original painting is in the Beaux-Arts de Paris, in Paris.

Table of Contents

TABLE OF CONTENTS

TABLE OF CONTENTS

TABLE OF CONTENTS

TABLE OF CONTENTS

Forward

Arabic Maccabees is the longest surviving book of Maccabees, however, does not appear to have originated as a book of Maccabees, but a pseudo-history book of the independent Kingdom of Judea from the Maccabean Revolt through the death of Herod the Great. The book concludes by claiming the story of Herod's son Antipater is in the book the author had previously written, which does not appear to have survived to the present. This lost book was probably not translated into Arabic like *Arabic Maccabees*, as it would have covered the era when Jesus was born, but probably did not mention him. The Arabic translation appears to have been made by a Christian, while the original text appears to have been written in Palestinean Aramaic by a Jewish woman, sometime in the mid 6th century AD.

The text only survives in Arabic, which is the reason it is named *Arabic Maccabees*. It is also known somewhat erroneously as *5th Maccabees*, based on the similar Syriac book of *5th Maccabees*, however, the Syriac book is simply a translation of Josephus' *The Judean War*. The title of *5th Maccabees* was introduced to the Arabic book by Anglican historian Henry Cotton in 1832, and picked up by other English authors, however, is not accurate. Josephus' *The Judean War* is considered extended canon in the Syriac Bibles under the name *5th Maccabees*, as well as the Ethiopic Bibles under its original name, while *Arabic Maccabees* is not considered canon in any bible.

The author appears to have intended the book as a 'Jewish' history book, which is often not dependent on historical facts. The author clearly had access to ancient sources, like Josephus' *Antiquities of the Judeans*, however, deviates from the older sources so often that the deviations cannot be errors. The author uses poetic terminology, such as referring to Judea as the 'Holy Land,' and Jerusalem as the 'city of the sacred temple,' giving the work a mythic quality. It suggests she intended the work for adolescents, unlike the earlier writers' works, which were intended for adults.

Most of the deviations from earlier works appear to be intended to make the Judean warriors and their allies seem more legendary, however, end up describing a strange alternate version of history. In *Arabic Maccabees*, Hannibal was the king of Carthage, who took his own life rather than face the humiliation of defeat. In reality, Hannibal was a general, who spoke in favor of the terms of surrender in front of the Carthaginian Senate after the armies of Carthage were defeated. In *Arabic Maccabees*, the Romans conquered the Parthians and ruled an empire reaching from the Atlantic to the Indus, and the Judeans conquered the Arabs of the Hejaz, not just the Nabateans of the Arabah.

Most of the content of the book is a retelling of the stories found in the Septuagint's *1ˢᵗ* and *2ⁿᵈ Maccabees* and Josephus' *Antiquities of the Judeans*, however, chapter 12 is only otherwise found *in Hebrew Maccabees*. Chapters 1 through 17 are remarkably similar to the content of *Hebrew Maccabees*, suggesting it was the primary source used by the author of *Arabic Maccabees* for the first third of the book. It is likely that the rest was reworked from some ancient source, and Jason of Cyrene, Justus of Tiberias, or Nicolaus of Damascus have all been proposed as sources as little of their work has survived to the present, although it was considered important during the Roman era. Although Jason's 5-volume *History of the Maccabees* was written in Cyrene, in modern Libya, and possibly in Judahite using the same Phoenician script that the Carthaginians used, it is unlikely he included Hannibal's invasion of Rome.

Justus of Tiberias was a 1ˢᵗ century Jewish historian who had been the secretary of King Herod Agrippa II, the last ruler from the Herodian dynasty who reigned over territories outside of Judea as a Roman client. Agrippa II fled Jerusalem in 66 AD, during the Judean uprising, and supported the Roman side in the First Judean-Roman War. His work has not survived to the present, however, Josephus mentioned in his autobiography that he was rebutting some of the claims of Justus in his *History of the Judean War*, meaning Justus' view of Josephus was not favorable. As Josephus had been a Judean general early in the war, Justus' view of him as one of the causes of the war would have been justified. According to Josephus' biography, he surrendered to the Romans after being trapped in a cave with his Judean soldiers, who didn't want to surrender to the Romans. He ordered a mass suicide, and then left the cave and surrendered to the Romans when his soldiers were dead. As this was Josephus' account, which he defended, Justus' account must have been far more scathing.

Although Justus had not been mentioned in Josephus' earlier *The Judean War*, Josephus wrote over 30 pages in his autobiography attacking Justus. He accused him of being one of the chief causes of the war, leading attacks on Greeks in Galilee before the war began, but then becoming noncommittal after the war had started, and ultimately served Agrippa on the Roman side. One of Josephus' claims was that Justus' *History of the Judean War* was filled with errors, but does not discuss them in detail. Josephus claimed that Justus' work lacked facts because Justus did not have access to the field notes of Vespasian and Titus, which suggests that Justus' work was written from the Judean perspective, and ignored the Roman perspective, unlike Josephus' work. Justus also wrote the *Chronicle of the Judean Kings*, which survived until the 9th century, but its content is unknown today. If it was also written from the Judean perspective, and not too dependent on facts, it is possible that the author of *Arabic Maccabees* used it as a source.

Nicolaus of Damascus was a Greek historian who lived in the 1st century BC and wrote the 144-volume *Universal History*, in which he attempted to unite the various mythical and historical sources of the ancient civilizations the Greeks had dominion over. *Universal History* does not survive to the present, however, excerpts and quotes from many books are known to exist, including books 2, 4, 5, 6, 7, 8, 96, 103, 104, 107, 108, 110, 114, 123 and 124. Josephus specifically referenced Nicolaus in *Antiquities of the Judeans*, and it is generally accepted that Josephus' *Antiquities of the Judeans* relied heavily on *Universal History* until the section dealing with the life of Herod Archelaus, where the writing style changes. Herod Archelaus was the king of Judea when Nicolaus died, and so *Universal History* would have ended part way through his reign, which is where *Antiquities of the Judeans* changed tone. However, if Josephus was relying heavily on Nicolaus' work, then the author of *Arabic Maccabees* could not have been, as the works report different events.

There is also a great deal of debate about the relation-ship between *Arabic Maccabees* and *Josippon*, a chronicle of Jewish history from Adam to the 1st century, ending during the reign of Emperor Titus. The origin of *Josippon* is debated, however, the anonymous author claims to be copying the ancient writings of Joseph ben Gorion (יוסף בן גוריון), which is generally assumed to be a reference to Josephus, however, Josephus' father's name was Matthias. The association of these two men named Joseph/Josephus first appeared in the scribal notes in a copy of the Latin language *On the Destruction of Jerusalem*. The 4th century book itself identifies a prefect in Jerusalem as Josephum Gorione Genitum, which the scribe claimed in the notes was Josephus. While the connection with Josephus is generally ignored by historians, *On the Destruction of Jerusalem* does support the existence of Joseph ben Gorion in Jerusalem during the same era as Josephus and Justus.

The *Josippon* became very popular in Western Europe after the invention of the printing press, which has led to a great deal of scholarly debate about its origin. European scholars have pulled the work apart and come to many conflicting views about its origin, however, generally agree it is a composite work, originally compiled in Hebrew in southern Italy in the 10th century, based on older Greek and Latin works, like the writings of Josephus and *On the Destruction of Jerusalem*. This original Josippon was then expanded by

Judah Leon ben Moses Mosconi in the 1300s before being printed in 1476. While the expansion by Mosconi is not debated, the origin of the Hebrew work is, as the Andalusian historian Abū Muḥammad Alī ibn Aḥmad ibn Saīd ibn Ḥazm had an Arabic translation of it, which he obtained from a Yemeni Jew.

Ibn Ḥazm was a prolific writer, who produced over 400 books before his death in 1064 BC, and his account is not doubted, so some scholars have suggested an earlier date for the original Hebrew work, in the 9th century. Alternatively, the 10th century Hebrew original may have been a translation of an older Arabic text. The Arabic name of the book ibn Ḥazm referred to, was called Ywsybws (يوسيبوس), which is an Arabic translit-eration of the Greek spelling of Josephus: Iôsêpos (Ἰώσηπος). This makes it unlikely that the Arabic trans-lation was made from the Hebrew *Josippon*, which claims to be a copy of the writing of 'Joseph ben Gorion,' which transliterates more directly as Ywsp bn Gwrywn (יוסף בן גוריון).

Scholars who hold the view that the Hebrew book is based on the Arabic book, often interpret the Arabic text as a translation of Hegesippus the Nazarene's work from the 2nd century. Hegesippus (Ἡγήσιππος) was the Greek name of a Nazarene scholar active in the 2nd century, who although being heretical to what later became

Orthodox Christianity, wrote against heresies of his day
by the Gnostics and of Marcion. Only quotes of Hegesippus' writing exist today, however, the idea that he
wrote a complete history of Christian events from the
death of Jesus until the late second century 'in five
volumes' comes from Jerome, writing circa 400 AD. The
earlier description by Eusebius circa 315 AD simply
reports that he wrote five books regarding Christian
theology, so Jerome may have confused Hegesippus' five
books with the 5-volume history of early Christianity
written by Papias circa 110 AD. As there are no reports
of Hegesippus writing a history of the Judean kings, any
connection between his writing a Arabic Maccabees
seems improbable.

If *Josippon* is a Hebrew translation of an Arabic translation of a Greek book by Josephus ben Gorion, then the
Greek original would have been written in the late 1st
century. In this case, the author of Arabic Maccabees
could have used it as a source, which would explain the
similarities. Arabic Maccabees was almost certainly
written in Palestinian Aramaic shortly after 525 AD,
however, the author clearly drew from Greek, Syriac,
and Coptic source texts. There are many anachronistic
Latin terms in Arabic Maccabees, which could indicate
Latin texts were used as well, however, all of the
borrowed Latin words had been adopted into Palestinian

Aramaic by the 6th century, so a Latin source cannot be proven.

The most obvious Latin loan word is ğntāyl (جنتايل), a translation of the Latin term gentilis, which was adopted by Arabic Christians before the time of Mohammed to refer to non-Jews. The original person documented as using this term in this way was Jerome (Eusebius Sophronius Hieronymus) when he created the original Vulgate, the Latin translation of the Orthodox Bible, in 382 AD. This indicates the Arabic translation of Maccabees was almost certainly made later than 382 AD, however, it is not clear if this term was in the original Palestinian Aramaic text.

Another obvious borrowed Latin term is dnānyr (دَنَانير), adopted from the Latin term denarius, which was the name of a common coin used in the Roman Empire from 211 BC to 244 AD. The word was also adopted into Greek as dênarion (δηνάριον), Syriac as dynrå (ܕܝܢܪܐ), and Palestinian Aramaic as dynr (דינרא). The denarius was a low-value coin, the name meant 'ten.' It was valued at 10 aes, the basic Roman monetary unit. While often compared to the cent or penny due to being made of copper, the aes coin was subdivided into smaller denominations, making the denarius the conceptual equivalent of a modern $10 or £10 bill. While the denarius was already in use by the era of the story, it was not in use in Greek-speaking countries. The original coin was likely the dekadrachm (δεκάδραχμον), a common ancient Greek coin valued at ten drachmas (δραχμή), the basic Greek monetary unit. As the name was adopted into Palestinian Aramaic and Syriac, as well as Arabic, it is unclear when the replacement of 'drachma' with 'dinar' took place, however, most of the drachmas used in the Middle East disappeared during Emperor Nero's monetary reforms of 64 AD, suggesting the term was replaced in the text sometime after that time.

One Latin term that was adopted into the Arabic text could be interpreted as support for the author using a Latin translation of 2nd Maccabees, the name Fylyks (فيليكس), in place of the name Philipos (Φιλιππος), used in the Septuagint's 2nd Maccabees. The Arabic name is derived from the Latin name Felix, meaning 'lucky,' which was adopted into many languages after the rise of Rome, including Greek as Phêlix (Φήλιξ), and Palestinian Aramaic as Flyks (פליקס).

Nevertheless, the reason for the substitution of Felix for Philip is not clear, as Philip was a popular Greek name, and easily translated into any language. It is possible that this is not derived from the Latin name Felix, but from Philip's Phrygian name, which is unattested. The Phrygian language was in decline for centuries by the era of Philip, and most Phrygians spoke a slang mixing Phrygian words into Greek, today known as Graeco-Phrygian. The Greek name Philippos (Φίλιππος) is a composite of phileô (φιλέω), meaning 'love,' and hippos (ἵππος), meaning horses. If this was based on his Graeco-Phrygian name, it could have been Phileś (Φιλεξ), combining the Greek phileô (φιλέω) with the New Phrygian eś (εξ), meaning 'horse' or 'donkey.'

If the author was using an older transliteration of the name than the translation found in the Septuagint, it suggests it was derived from a non-Greek text, possibly Jason of Cyrene's 5-volume *History of the Maccabees*, which the author of the Septuagint's *2ⁿᵈ Maccabees* claimed to be abridging. The Septuagint's *2ⁿᵈ Maccabees* includes a long preface before the 'bridged' version of Jason's work, however, it is not clear if the preface was written in Greek when the Greek translation was prepared, or earlier when an abridged copy of Jason's work was prepared, and then translated into Greek with the abridged book.

The preface also included a transliteration of a Judahite word in an otherwise unknown quote attributed to Jeremiah, indicating the Greek translator did not understand the reference, which suggests it had been transliterated directly into an Aramaic precursor to the Septuagint's *2ⁿᵈ Maccabees*. If Phileś (Φιλεξ) was transliterated into Aramaic, it would have likely been spelled as Fylyś (ℨ^ᒪ^ʔ), which could be either translated into Greek as the name Philippos or be interpreted as the Latin name Felix. As a result, it is not clear whether the name of 'Philip' from the *Septuagint* was changed to Felix in an interim Latin translation, or if it was the original name, better preserved in an Aramaic text the author had access to.

Fortunately, the evidence of the Greek source texts is easier to determine. One clear demonstration is the city of Aleppo, in northern Syria, being called Hlbws (حلبوس). The Arabic name is Ḥalab (حلب), so the Arabic translator could not have recognized the name and simply transliterated the name in the source text. The Arabic name is a transliteration of the Greek name Chalibôs (Χαλιβώς), an ancient Greek spelling of the name of Aleppo. As any Greek-to-Arabic translator could have looked up the meaning of Chalibôs (Χαλιβώς), the name must have already been transliterated into another language. In this case, the author appears to have simply transliterated the old Greek name directly into Palestinian Aramaic as Hlbws (חלבוס), confounding the later Aramaic-to-Arabic translator.

A similar odd transliteration provides evidence of the Palestinian Aramaic source text the Arabic translator used. The name ḥōrāk (حعراك) is used as a reference to the Parthian capital in a story set in 40 BC. In 58 BC, the capital of the Parthian empire was moved to Ctesiphon (Κτησιφῶν), near modern Baghdad in central Iraq, indicating that this was an odd spelling of 'Iraq.' The name 'Iraq' is accepted as having been used since at least the Persian era, as airga (𐎡𐎼𐎥), meaning 'lowlands,' however, the proper Arabic spelling of 'Iraq' is āl-ôrāq (العراق), meaning 'the Iraq.' In this case, the name has been transliterated directly into Arabic from the Palestinian Aramaic hÔråq (העיראק), meaning 'the Iraq.' While this could also be interpreted as evidence the author wrote in Hebrew, the plural form of ḥōrākyn (حعـراكين) is later used, a transliteration of hÔråqyn (העיראקין), meaning 'the Iraqis' in Palestinian Aramaic, but not in Hebrew, which would have rendered the word as hÔråqym (העיראקים). Similarly, it eliminates Syriac as the author's language, as in Syriac the names would have been written as Ôyråq (ܐܘܪܩ) and dÔyråqån (ܕܐܘܪܩܢ).

Like the language, the era the original work was written can be identified based on the strange commentary the author provides about calendars. The author claims that the Julian calendar started in the year that Herod became king of Judea. The Julian calendar was introduced by Julius Caesar in 45 BC, however, Herod became king in 37 BC, meaning that the calendar is off by 8 years. The only time when someone could have made such an obvious error would have been shortly after 525 AD, as there was an 8-year gap in Greek, Latin, and Syriac Christian calendars when the calculations of Dionysius Exiguus were adopted.

Prior to 525, different Christian churches used the calculations of either Panodoros of Alexandria or Annianus of Alexandria to determine the Incarnation of Jesus. Both of these calculations were made circa 400 AD and differed by six months based on different interpretations of the Gospels. This was resolved in 525 when Dionysius Exiguus redid the calculations after it was decided that Jesus was not incarnated, and determined that the Annunciation of Jesus was 8 or 7.5 years earlier than previously accepted. The Orthodox Tewahedo churches continue to use a calendar that is 7.5 years off of the Julian calendar to denote the Incarnation of Jesus, based on the calculations of Annianus of Alexandria. While this can be used to date the Palestinian Aramaic authorship to shortly after 525 AD, it also confirms that she was a Jew, as there would be no reason for a Christian to think that the Julian calendar of the Roman Empire was based on Herod becoming king of Judea. However, the use of the Julian calendar, and the reference to the 8-year gap, also indicates she was living in the Byzantine Empire.

There are several indicators in the text that the original author was a woman, including the significant role the women played in the book, the fact that the book is anonymous, and the matter-of-fact way that male homosexuality was treated. In most of the ancient Israelite, Judahite, and Christian texts, women play a minor role, if they have any role, however, this is not because they were not significant in their time. In the 600s BC, the prophet Ezekiel referred to King Zedekiah's mother Hamutal as a 'lioness,' however, no stories survive that explain why she would be viewed that way. The author of *Arabic Maccabees* has women playing a major role throughout the latter section of the book, dealing with the later Hasmonean kings and the rise and fall of Herod.

The only time the author glosses over a significant historical woman is in the case of Aristobulus I's mother. Aristobulus I was the first Judean High Priest to establish a completely independent Judea, becoming its first king. His father, known as John in the *Septuagint*, but Hyrcanus in *Arabic Maccabees* and Josephus' *The Judean War*, was High Priest in Jerusalem, and the general who established the autonymous government of Judea within the Selucid's crumbling empire. According to Josephus, when he died, his will was that his son Aristobulus should follow him as High Priest, while his wife should be the secular ruler of Judea. Instead, Aristobulus imprisoned his mother and seized the throne. Instead of becoming the first monarch of an independent Judea, she starved to death in a prison cell.

The author reports that he imprisoned her, but claims it was because he did not like his brother Alexander, who would eventually become king after he died. The fate of his mother is not mentioned. Like Josephus, the author does not name the woman and calls her husband John by the name Hyrcanus. Based on this and many other similarities between this book and Josephus' writing, it is clear the author used him as a source. Nevertheless, she chose to not include Aristobulus' matricide.

The point of the book appears to be a retelling of the rise and fall of the Hasmoneans, not just as a dynasty, but also what happened after Herod seized control of the kingdom. It ends with Herod's downfall and death, which is largely caused by the friction between the women in his life. He had two wives, his first was an Edomite named Dosithea, and his second was a Hasmonean princess named Mariamne. The author describes Mariamne as a saint, who was wrongfully murdered by Herod due to the machinations of his sister. At the time, Herod and Mariamne's two sons were in Rome, studying Latin and Roman customs, and after killing Mariamne, he appointed his son Antipater by

Dosithea as heir to the kingdom. While Dosithea is not described as being part of the plot to place Antipater on the throne, both Herod's sister and brother are involved, suggesting his Edomite family did not want his eldest son Antipater to be sidelined for a more 'noble' son by a Hasmonean princess. The execution of the saintly Mariamne caused an irreconcilable division between Herod and his sons by Mariamne, ultimately leading to his executing them by crucifixion on a gibbet. This ended the Hasmonean line, and his Edomite son Antipater followed him as king.

The author also describes her brother Aristobulus as being saintly, whom Herod also had killed a few years earlier. The author's treatment of Aristobulus also supports her being a woman, as a man would have probably left out the homosexual desires that Gellius the Roman servant of Mark Antony felt towards Aristobulus. By the era the book must have been written, homophobia had become the norm in Jewish society and was growing within the larger Christian community of the Byzantine Empire. Given all of the other alterations in the book, it is unlikely that this detail would have been included if the author thought he might be accused of being a homosexual himself. However, this would not have been an issue for a female writer.

Her treatment of Gellius' view of Aristobulus is also complicated by Gellius' claim that Aristobulus must be the son of an angel who impregnated his mother. The author reports that Aristobulus and his sister Mariamne looked the same, and she was very beautiful, which suggests Aristobulus was effeminate, but also implies they both would have been viewed as 'angelic.' Combined with them being described as saintly, the 'angelic' siblings appear to be similar to the Byzantine view of Jesus and may have been influenced by it.

It is unlikely that Gellius would have been referring to the Middle Eastern concept of a divine messenger, however, he may have been referring to Mercury, the messenger of Jupiter. However, this interpretation is somewhat unlikely, as Mercury was only adopted into the Roman pantheon in the 3rd century BC, and there are no references to him mating with humans. This story is set less than a century after Mercury was adopted, and therefore a reference to Mercury impregnating a woman wouldn't have made sense to a Roman. Similar stories of the gods impregnating humans to create exceptional humans can be found in the Middle East going back to at least the Neo-Sumerian era, and are also found in Greek mythology, so it's possible Gellius was referring to this. However, it is more likely that this concept originated in the writing of a Jew, as the concept of human-angel hybrids is found in the Torah.

The point of adding the 'angelic' aspect to Aristobulus may have been to create a gloss for children, who would not have understood why Gellius was painting pictures of Aristobulus, and writing letters about how beautiful he was to Mark Antony. Overall, the work appears to be written for adolescents and was not intended to be taken as a serious history. The fact that the Romans always won their wars in the book, establishing an empire from the Atlantic to India suggests that the author was attempting to mitigate the fall of Jerusalem by claiming it was the will of God that the Romans should rule everything. This seems to be confirmed in chapter 12, where either the author or Arabic translator refers to the rise of Rome as the fourth empire prophesied by Daniel. Daniel is not generally accepted as a prophet by Jews and was not popular enough for his entire book to be translated into Hebrew by the Hasmonean dynasty, resulting in the Masoretic version being a mix of Hebrew and Aramaic chapters.

However, if the author did believe the idea that Daniel had predicted the rise of a fourth empire, and it was Rome, it would mean that the fall of Jerusalem was caused by the Jews fighting against the will of God. As her earlier work began with the reign of Herod's son

Antipater, it is likely it dealt with the fall of Jerusalem, and if its conclusion that this was 'by the will of God,' Daniel's prophecy could have served as the basis of that conclusion.

The Arabic translator left notes directly in the translation, which sometimes makes it difficult to determine who is speaking, the author or the translator. Sometimes the notes are obvious, such as when the translator added 'the author claims,' however, others can only be theorized about based on the inconsistency of the writing style. At one point, in chapter 55, the translator seems to dismiss the author's claims about the balsam plants of Jericho, however, ancient sources agree with the author's core claims about the plants only growing in Jericho before the fall of Jerusalem.

One obvious error indicates the Arabic translator was a Christian, which is the substitution of the name 'Pilate' for 'Herod' found in chapter 59. Based on the context, it is clear that Herod is who is being referenced, however, the name bylāts (بيلاطس) appears in the text, the Arabic translation of 'Pilate.' This is not a scribal error that a Jew would have made, as Pontus Pilate played no significant role in Jewish history. Pilate is famous in Christianity for being the one who sentenced Jesus to death, while Herod is famous for ordering all the male babies in Bethlehem to be killed. Mixing these two up is not uncommon for Christians. Pilate is also famous among Samaritans for leading an attack on the temple on Mount Gerisom, where he claimed the Samaritans were hiding some sacred relics of Moses, however, the focus of the book is Judean history, and therefore a Samaritan author is unlikely. Additionally, the author refers to the Torah and Tanakh (Christian Old Testament) by the phrase '24 books,' indicating she was a Jew, not a Samaritan, as the Samaritans do not use the Tanakh.

The existing Arabic translation also includes the Islamic phrase 'peace be upon him' in chapter 12, which is an honorific for the dead prophets. This is either evidence that chapter 12 was a copy of something from an Arabic book the translator added, or an indicator that the translation took place after Islam had become dominant in the region, and Islamic phrases had become common. In any event, the Arabic translation probably took place during or before the Crusades, as both Jews and Christians in Palestine and Jordan had adopted Arabic by the year 1200.

Chapter 1

It was ordained by the kings of the Greek gentiles[1] that large sums of money should be sent into the holy city every year, and should be delivered to the priests, that they might add it to the treasury of the temple of God, as money for the receivers of alms and widows.

Seleucus[2] was king of Macedonia[3] and he had a friend, one of his captains, who was called Heliodorus. This man was sent to plunder the treasury, and to take whatever money was there. When this was heard abroad, it created great grief among the citizens, and they were afraid in case Heliodorus should go further, as they did not have the power to stop him from executing his orders. Therefore they all called to God for aid, and ordained a general fast, and supplicated with humility, bowing their knees, wailing greatly, putting on sackcloth, and rolling themselves in ashes. Onias the high priest and the other princes and elders did this, as well as the common people, including women and children.

The next day Heliodorus came into the temple of God, with a train of followers, and entered into the temple with his foot soldiers, he himself being on horseback, and searched for the money. But the great and good God sent a loud, terrible noise upon him, and he saw a person armed with weapons of war, riding on a large horse, and advancing against him. He was seized with fear and trembling, and that person came up to him, and pulled him off from his saddle, knocking him violently to the ground. He was dumbfounded in terror and frightened out of his senses. When his attendants saw what had happened to him, but could see no one who had done these things unto him, they carried him to his house as quickly as possible, where he remained for several days, neither speaking nor eating any food.

During this time, the chief men among his friends went to Onias, the priest, begging him to implore the great and good God that He would not punish him. Onias did this, and Heliodorus was healed of his disease. Then he saw in a vision the person, whom he had seen in the sanctuary, commanding him to go to Onias the priest, and to salute him, and honor him, telling him, that the great and good God had heard his prayers, and had healed him at Onias' request. Heliodorus rushed to Onias the priest, whom he bowed down before, and gave him money of various kinds to add to the treasury.

Then he traveled from Jerusalem into the country of Macedonia and told King Seleucus what had happened to him, begging that he would not compel him to become his representative in Jerusalem. The king wondered at the things that Heliodorus told him and commanded him to tell them to the world. He took care that his men should be removed from Jerusalem, and increased the gifts that he sent there annually, on account of what had happened to Heliodorus. The kings added more to the money which they ordered to be given to the priests, that it might be spent on the orphans and widows, and also to that which was to be spent on the sacrifices.

Chapter 1 Notes

1 Arabic: ğntāyl (جنتايل)

The Arabic word is a translation of the Latin term gentilis, which was adopted by Arabic Christians before the time of Mohammed to refer to non-Jews. The original person to have used this term in any significant way was Jerome (Eusebius Sophronius Hieronymus) when he created the original Vulgate, the Latin translation of the Orthodox Bible, in 382 AD. This indicates the Arabic translation of Maccabees was almost certainly made later than 382 AD.

2 Arabic: slwqs (سلوقس). Translation: Seleucus

Seleucus IV Philopator (Σέλευκος Φιλοπάτωρ) was the king of the Seleucid Empire from 187 to 175 BC. At that time, the empire covered modern day Syria, Lebanon, Israel, Palestine, Iraq, Kuwait, southwestern Turkey, and western Iran.

3 Arabic: mqdwnyā (مقدونيا)

Seleucus IV Philopator never ruled over Macedonia. This suggests a misinterpretation by the Arabic translator.

Chapter 2

There was a Macedonian named Ptolemy,[1] endowed with knowledge and understanding, who lived in Egypt, and so the Egyptians made him king of Egypt. He possessed the desire to seek out diverse wisdom and collected all the books of wise men from every region.[2]

Being eager to obtain the twenty-four books,[3] he wrote to the high priest in Jerusalem, requesting he send him seventy elders from among those who were most skilled in those books. He sent a gift to the priest with the letter. When the king's letter arrived, the priest chose seventy learned men, and sent them, together with a man named Eleazar, one excelling in religion, science, and philosophy, who departed for Egypt. When the king heard they were coming, he commanded seventy houses to be prepared, and the men to lodge there. He also ordered a secretary to be appointed for each one, who would write down the interpretation of these books in the Greek alphabet and language. He forbade anyone of these men from communicating with any of the others, so they could not conspire to make any change in those books.

The secretaries wrote down from each of them a translation of the twenty-four books, and when the translations were finished, Eleazar brought them to the king. He compared them in the king's presence and found they agreed, for which the king was exceeding glad, and ordered a large sum of money to be divided among the party. However, for Eleazar himself he rewarded with a a much greater gift; on that day he set free every slave which was found in Egypt, from the tribe of Judah and of Benjamin, so they might return to their own country in Syria.[4] There were around one hundred and thirty thousand of them. Additionally, he ordered money to be distributed among them, so that several dinars[5] were given to each person, who, after receiving this, left for their own land.

Then he commanded a great table to be made of the purest gold, which should be large enough to contain a representation of the whole land of Egypt, and a picture of the Nile, from the origin of its stream to its end in Egypt, with its various divisions in the country, and how it drains the whole land. He also ordered the table to be set with many precious stones, this table was made, and its carving was finished, and it was set with precious stones. It was carried into the city of Jerusalem, a present to the magnificent temple. Arriving in safety, it was placed in the temple by the king's command. Never before had men beheld its like, the beauty of the images, and the excellence of the workmanship.

Chapter 2 Notes

1 Arabic: btlymws (بَطْلِيمُوس). Translation: Ptolemy

Ptolemy I Soter (Πτολεμαῖος Σωτήρ) was the Macedonian general who was appointed satrap of Egypt at the Partition of Babylon, in 323 BC. After the imperial regent Perdiccas was killed in 321 BC, Ptolemy was offered the regency of the Macedonian empire until Alexander III's son was old enough to assume the kingship, however, rejected the offer. At the time, the empire was on the verge of collapse, and in the ensuing wars of the Diadochi, Ptolemy managed to secure his kingship over Egypt, Cyrene, Judea, Syria, Cyprus, and Cilicia.

2 General Ptolemy was viewed as a wise man, however, he is not generally believed to have founded the Library of Alexandria, which is attributed to his son Ptolemy II Philadelphus, who ruled Egypt between 284 and 246 BC. During Philadelphus' reign, the wealth of Ptolemy's Egypt was at its height, and he ordered the building of the Mouseion of Alexandria, an early university that included the more famous Library of Alexandria, where tens of thousands of ancient documents were translated into Greek.

3 The term "twenty-four books" refers to the Torah and Tanakh, which is considered the Jewish Bible. The Greek version of this collection of books, known as the Septuagint, meaning "seventy," included more texts than the Hebrew version. However, the number of texts included in the Septuagint varied over time. The earlier versions of the

Septuagint might have included several books attributed to Enoch, Methuselah, and Lamech. Some fragments of these books were found among the Dead Sea Scrolls. Other books that were likely once included, but removed by Christians, would have been the apocalyptic books attributed to the prophet Ezra, Daniel, and Azariah, as well as the other texts attributed to Jeremiah and Baruch. Many of these texts survive in Ge'ez translations, which appear to have previously been translated into Greek.

The shorter Hebrew collection was standardized by Simon the Zealot, high priest/king of the Hasmonean Dynasty of Judea between 140 and 134 BC. The much shorter Samaritan collection is believed to have been reconstructed by the Samaritans from Jewish sources after General Pompey liberated them from Judean slavery in 63 BC.

The fact that the Arabic translator refers to the "twenty-four books," supports the translator being a Palestinian Christian after the rise of the Byzantine Church, as the Palestinian Christians generally preferred the Hebrew translation over the Greek.

4 Arabic: swryā (سُورِيَّا)

Under the rule of the Persian Empire, Macedonian Empire, and the Ptolemys' empire, Judea was the southern region of the satrapy of Syria. This suggests the Arabic translator was using an old manuscript as a source, regardless of the errors in the interpretation of who the Macedonians and Greeks were.

5 Arabic: dnānyr (دَنَانِير). Translation: dinars

The Arabic word was adopted from the Latin term denarius, which was the name of a common coin used in the Roman Empire from 211 BC to 244 AD. The word was also adopted into Greek as dênarion (δηνάριον), Syriac as dynrå (ܕܝܢܪܐ), and Palestinian Aramaic as dynr (דינרא). The denarius was a low-value coin, the name translating as 'ten.' It was valued at 10 aes, the basic Roman monetary unit. While often compared to the cent or penny due to being made of copper, the aes coin was subdivided into smaller denominations, making the denarius the conceptual equivalent of a modern $10 or £10 bill. While the denarius was already in use by the era of the story, it was not in use in Greek-speaking countries. The original coin was likely the dekadrachm (δεκάδραχμον), a common ancient Greek coin valued at ten drachmas (δραχμή), the basic Greek monetary unit.

Chapter 3

There was a Macedonian King named Antiochus,[1] who, after the death of the previously mentioned Ptolemy, the king of Egypt, took his armies to attack the second Ptolemy. Having conquered and slain Ptolemy, he conquered the country of Egypt and took ownership of it. From there, as his fame grew, and he subdued a great part of the earth, with the kings of Persia and others paying homage to him.

After this his heart was lifted up, and being puffed up with pride, he commanded images to be made after his own likeness so men could worship them, and praise and honor him. When these were made, he sent messengers into all the regions of his empire, commanding them to be worshipped and adored. The Gentiles agreed to this command, fearing and dreading his tyranny.

There were at that time in Judaea three men, the very worst of all mortals, and each of them had, as it were, a connexion in the same sort of vice. The name of these three were Menelaus, Simeon, and Alcimnss. About that time, there appeared certain images, which the citizens of Jerusalem saw in the air for the space of forty days. They were the appearances of men riding on fiery horses fighting with each other. So those impious men went to Antiochus, to obtain from him some authority, that they might perpetrate with ease whatever they wished, of whoredom, and the stealing of men's property, and in short, that they might rule over the rest, and might keep them in subjection.

And they said to him, "Oh king, there have appeared recently in the air over Jerusalem fiery horsemen, fighting with each other, and on that account the Hebrews have rejoiced, saying, that this foretells the death of King Antiochus."

The king believed this and was filled with rage. He marched to Jerusalem as rapidly as possible and arrived before the people had heard he was coming. His men attacked the inhabitants and slaughtered them with the sword in great numbers. They also wounded many, and a great number they captured as slaves. Some escaped and fled into the mountains and forests, where they survived a long time by eating plants.

After this, Antiochus decided to leave the country. But the evil that he had done to the people did not satisfy him, so he left as his representative a man named Philip,[2] ordering him to force the Judeans to worship his image and to eat pork. Philip did this, ordering the people to obey the king in all things he had commanded him. However, many refused to do the things they were ordered to do, so he slaughtered a great multitude of them. Those wicked wretches who followed the king's commands he saved, along with their families, and raised their status.

Chapter 3 Notes

1 Arabic: ȯntywḫws (أنطيوخوس). Translation: Antiochus

The history of this chapter is counterfactual, as is much of the book. It was Antiochus III who defeated the armies of Ptolemy V in the Battle of Panium in 200 AD and took control of Syria, including Judea. Antiochus III did not launch an invasion of Egypt itself, as Rome had agreed to protect Egypt. Antiochus III had also reconquered the rebelling regions of Bactria and Persia before his invasion of Egypt.

2 Arabic: fylyks (فيليكس). Translation: Felix

This story is also told in the Setuagint's 2nd Maccabees, where 'Felix' is named Philip a man descended from Phrygia (Φιλιππον το μεν γενος Φρυγα). Felix was a Latin name, meaning 'lucky,' which was adopted into many languages after the rise of Rome, including Greek as Phêlix (Φήλιξ), Palestinian Aramaic as Flyks (פליקס), and Arabic Fylyks (فيليكس). Felix was not used in Greek or Phygian at the time the story was set, and so the name 'Philip' is imported from 2nd Maccabees. This name may either be read as evidence of a Latin copy of 2nd Maccabees being used as a source text, or evidence that Philip's Graeco-Phrygian name was Philés (Φιλεξ), which means the same thing as the Greek Philippos (Φίλιππος).

Chapter 4

Afterward, Eleazar was seized, he who had gone with the doctors to Ptolemy, and was then a very old man of ninety years. He was brought before Philip, who said to him, "Eleazar, truly you are a wise and prudent man. I have loved you for many years, and therefore I do not wish your death. Therefore, obey the king, and worship his image, and eat of his sacrifices, and leave in safety."

Eleazar replied to him, "I am not about to forsake my obedience to God, in order to obey the king."

Philip approached him and whispered, "Quietly send someone to bring you meat from your own offerings and place it on my table. Eat some of that in the presence of the people, that they may know that you have obeyed the king, and you will save your life. No harm will have been done to your religion."

Eleazar answered him, "I do not obey God under any kind of fraud, but rather I will endure your violence. As I am an old man of ninety years, my bones are now weakened, and my body has wasted away. If I will therefore endure these torments with a brave spirit, from which even the bravest young men shrink back in fear, my people and the youths of my people will bravely imitate me and will say, 'How is it that we may not endure the pains, which one who is inferior to us in strength, and less substantial in flesh and bones has undergone?' which indeed will be better for me, than to deceive them by feigned obedience to the king. Then they would say, 'If that decrepit old man, wise and prudent as he is, is clinging to life and overcome by the pain of temporary matters is abandoning his religion, then it would be lawful for us if it is lawful for him since he is an old man and a wise one, and one whom we ought to follow.' I would rather die, leaving to them a constancy in religion and patience against tyranny, than live after having weakened their faith in obeying their Lord and following his commands, so that through me they may achieve happiness and not misery."

When Philip heard the determination of Eleazar, he was violently enraged with him and commanded him to be tortured in a variety of ways, so that he came into the most desperate mortal struggle, and said, "Oh God, you know that I might have saved myself from the troubles into which I have fallen by obeying someone other than you. This, however, I have not done, but I have chosen to obey you, and have considered all the violence against me as nothing, for the sake of constancy in obedience to you. Now, I think little of the things that have happened to me according to your pleasure and support them as well as I can. I therefore pray to you, that you will accept this from me, and cause me to die before I become weaker in endurance."

CHAPTER 4

God heard his prayers and immediately he died, but he left his people devoted to the worship of their God, filled with faith, consistent in religion, and ready to survive the trials that awaited them.

Chapter 5

The story of the death of the seven brothers.

After this, seven brothers were seized, along with their mother, and they were sent to the king, as he had not yet gone far from Jerusalem. When they had been taken to the king, one of them was brought into his presence, whom he had ordered to renounce his religion, and he said to him, "If you think you can introduce a truth to us, this is not the case. We have learned truth from our fathers, and have bound ourselves to embrace the worship of God alone and constantly follow the law. We will not stop doing this."

King Antiochus was angry at these words, and commanded an iron frying pan to be brought, and to be placed on the fire. Then he ordered the young man's tongue to be cut out, and his hands and feet to be cut off, and the skin of his head to be flayed off, and to be placed in the pan, and they this. Then he commanded a large brazen caldron to be brought and set over the fire, into which the rest of his body was thrown. And when the man was near dying, he ordered the fire to be removed from him, that he might be tortured the longer, intending to terrify his mother and brothers. However, this gave them additional courage and strength, to maintain their religion with constancy, and to bear all those torments which tyranny could inflict upon them.

When the first was dead, the second was brought before him, to whom some of the attendants advised, "Obey the orders which the king will give you, or you will die like your brother."

He replied, "I am not weaker in spirit than my brother, nor less than him in my faith. Bring forward your fire and sword, and do not do less than that which you did to my brother."

They did to him as had been done to his brother, and he called out to the king, "Hear, you monster of cruelty towards men, and know that you gain nothing of ours except our bodies. Our minds you will not gain, and these will soon go to their Creator, He who will restore them to their bodies when He shall resurrect the dead men of his nation and the slain ones of his people."

The third was brought out, who beckoning with his hand said to the king, "Why do you frighten us, enemy? Know that this is ordained upon us from heaven, which we undergo while giving thanks to God, and from Him we hope for our reward."

The king, and those who stood near him, admired the courage of the youth, and the firmness of his mind, and his reasoned argument. The king commanded that he be killed.

The fourth was brought out, who said, "For God's religion we have enslaved our bodies, and rent them out so we may require payment from Him, on that day when you will have no excuse, in the judgment, and you will not be able to endure your tortures."

The king commanded that he be killed.

The fifth was brought out, who said to him, "Don't think to yourself that God has forgotten us because of the things which He has sent upon us. But truly his will is to honor us, and loving sends these things. He will avenge us against you and your descendants."

The king commanded that he be killed.

The sixth was brought out, who said, "I confess my offenses to God, but I believe that they shall be forgiven me through my death. You have now opposed God by slaying those who embrace His religion, and surely He will repay you according to your deeds, and will root you out from his earth."

The king commanded that he be killed.

The seventh was brought out, who was a boy. Then his mother got up, fearless and unmoved, and looked upon the corpses of her children, and she said, "My sons, I don't know how I conceived each one of you, or when I conceived him. Nor had I the power of giving him breath, or of bringing him out into the light of this world, or of bestowing on him courage and understanding, but the great and good God himself formed him according to his own will, and gave him a form that he liked, and brought him into the world through his power, appointing to him a term of life, and good rules, and a dispensation of religion, as it pleased Him. But you now have sold to God your bodies which he himself formed, and your souls which he created, and you have accepted the judgments which he decreed. Therefore you are happy in the things which happily you have obtained, and blessed for the things in which you have been victorious."

When Antiochus saw her get up, he supposed that she had done this through being overcome by fear for her child, and he thought that she was about to tell him to be obedient to the king, so he might not die like his brothers. But when he heard her words, he was ashamed, and blushed, and commanded the boy to be brought to him, so he might exhort him, and persuade him to love life and deter him from death, in case all of them should be seen opposing his authority and others should follow their example. Therefore, when he was brought to him, he spoke with him, promised him riches, and swore to him that he would make him his viceroy. But when the boy was not at all moved by his words, and paid no attention to them. The king turned to his mother, and said, "Happy woman, pity your son, the last you have surviving, and tell him to comply with my orders and to escape the suffering that has happened to his brothers."

She replied, "Bring him here so I may tell him the words of God."

When they had brought him to her, she went aside from the crowd, then she kissed him, and mocked the things that Antiochus had said to her, and said to him, "My son, be obedient to me, because I have birthed you, and suckled you, and educated you, and taught you the divine religion. Look up now to the heaven, and see the earth, and the water, and the fire, and understand that the one true God himself created these. He formed man of flesh and blood, who lives a short time, and then will die. Therefore fear the true God, who does not die, and obey the true being, who does not change his promises. Don't fear this mere giant, but die for God's religion like your brothers have died. For if you could see, my son, their honorable dwelling place, and the light of their habitation, and to what glory they have attained, you would not consider not following them. Honestly, I also hope that the great and good God has ordained that I will follow quickly behind you."

CHAPTER 5

Then the boy stated, "Know that I will obey God, and will not obey the commands of Antiochus. Therefore, don't delay me from following my brothers. Don't hinder me from going to the place where they have gone."

He said to the king, "Woe to you from God! Where will you hide from Him? Where will you seek refuge? Whose help will you implore, that He will not take vengeance on you? Truly you have done us a kindness when you had planned to do us evil, you have done evil to your own mind, and have destroyed it, while you have planned to do good for it. Now we are on our way to a life where death can never follow, and will live in light where darkness can never overcome. Your dwelling will be in the infernal regions, with exquisite punishments from God. I trust, that the wrath of God will depart from his people on account of what we have suffered for them, but you, He will torment in this world, and bring you to a wretched death. Then you will go into eternal torments."

Antiochus was angry, seeing that the boy opposed his authority, and he commanded him to be tortured even more than his brothers. This was done, and he died. But their mother intreated God, and preyed to Him that she might follow her sons, and immediately she died. Then Antiochus departed to return to his country Macedonia, and he wrote to Philip, and the other governors in Syria, that they should slaughter all the Jews, except those who embraced his religion. His servants obeyed his command, putting many men to death.

Chapter 6

John[1] fled to one of the mountains which was fortified, and the men who were scattered around rallied to him, but some concealed themselves in hidden places.

After that, when Antiochus had traveled a greater distance from the country, Mattathias sent his son Judas secretly into the cities of Judea, to inspect them and learn of his people's health, and to inspire as many as possible with courage and zeal for religion. He suggested that they send their wives and their children to him.

Some of the nobles among them, who had remained behind, went out to him, and said, "Nothing is left for us, but prayer to God, and confidence in Him, and a fight with our enemies. Perhaps God will give us assistance and victory over them." Then the people assented to the opinion of Mattathias, and they followed it.

Philip heard of this, and he marched against them with a great army. While marching, he heard that a thousand Judeans, both men and women, had assembled and were living in a certain cave, so they could continue their own way of worship. He turned aside to them with some of his troops, sending the commanders of his men with the rest of the army against Mattathias. Philip demanded from those who were in the cave, that they should come out to him, and consent to convert to his religion, but they refused. When he threatened that he would smoke them out, they ignored it and did not come out to him. He put smoke into the cave, and they all died.

When the generals of his army were marching against Mattathias, and as they approached him and were preparing for battle, one of the generals, of noble blood, went to him and proposed he obey the king and not oppose his authority, so that he and those with him might survive. To which he replied, "I obey God the true king, but you obey your king, and do whatever seems good to you." Then he stopped speaking, and they began to plot against him.

A certain despicable man, one of the worst of the Judeans was with them, and he encouraged them to turn against him and attack him. Mattathias rushed at him with his sword drawn and cut off the Judean's head. Then he attacked the general, for whom the Judean was speaking, and killed him as well.

Mattathias' companions, seeing what he had done, rallied to him, and they burst into the camp of the enemies, slaughtering great numbers of them, and caused them to flee. Afterward, they pursued the fugitives until they had killed all of them.

After this, Mattathias blew the trumpet and proclaimed an expedition against Philip. He and his companions entered into the land of Judah and captured many of their cities. The highest God gave them safety through his hands, from the generals of Antiochus, and they returned to observing their religion. The bands of their enemies retreated from before them.

Chapter 6 Notes

1 Arabic: ywhnā (يُوحَنَّا). Translation: John

Based on comparison to the Greek and Hebrew books of Maccabees, this is likely a scribal error. The other books report that 'Mattathias the son of John' fled to Modi'in. After this brief reference, John disappears, and Mattathias appears as the protagonist of the chapter.

Chapter 7

Mattathias became infirm, and when he was near death, he called his five sons, and said, "I am certain that many great wars will be kindled in the land of Judea as the great and good God has stirred us up to wage war against our enemies. I command you to fear God and trust in him, and be zealous of the law, and the temple, and the people also. Prepare yourselves to wage war against its enemies, and don't fear dying, because, without doubt, this is decreed for all men. If God makes you victorious, you will immediately obtain that which you seek, but if you fall, you still will not lose in his sight."

Mattathias died and was buried, and his sons did what he had commanded them. They agreed to make their brother Judas their leader. Judas their brother was the wisest and bravest of them all. An army was sent against them by Philip, commanded by a man called Seron, whom Judas with his company forced to retreat, and he slaughtered great numbers. The fame of Judas became known abroad and increased greatly in the ears of men. All the nations that were around him feared him greatly.

King Antiochus was told what Mattathias and his son Judas had done. News of this also reached the king of the Parthians, and so he broke his alliance with Antiochus, ending their friendship, and following the example of Judas.

This caused Antiochus a great deal of stress, and he called one of his trusted officers named Lysias, a stout and brave man, and said to him, "I have decided to go to Parthia to make war, and I wish to leave behind my son in my place. I will take half of my army, and leave the rest with my son, and know that I have given you the governance of my son, and the regent of the men I leave with him. You know well what Mattathias and Judas have done to my friends and my subjects. Therefore, send a powerful army into the land of Judea, and attack the land of Judea with the sword to root them out, to demolish their dwellings, and to destroy all traces of them."

Antiochus departed for Parthia, and Lysias prepared three strong and brave generals, skilled in war. One was named Ptolemy, the second was Nicanor, and the third was Gorgias. With them, he sent forty thousand of the best infantry and seven thousand cavalry. He also ordered them to bring Syrian and Palestinian auxiliaries and to root out the Judeans entirely. They marched out, leading a multitude of merchants that they might sell the slaves they were about to capture from among the Judeans.

Reports of this reached Judas the son of Mattathias, and he went to the temple of the great and good God and assembled his men, and advised them to fast, make sacrifices, and pray to the great and good God, and ordered that they should pray to Him for victory against their enemies. This they did.

After this, Judas organized his men, and appointed a chief over each thousand, and each hundred, and each fifty, and each ten. Then he commanded a proclamation to be made by trumpet throughout his army, that whoever was afraid, and whoever God commanded to be dismissed from the army, should go home. Great numbers left, but there remained with him seven thousand strong and brave men, skilled experienced warriors. These did not flee but marched against their enemies.

When they had approached them, Judas prayed to his Lord, begging Him that He would turn away the malice of his enemy. and that He would assist him, and give him victory. Then he commanded the priests to sound the trumpets, which they did, and all his men called upon God and charged the army of Nicanor. God gave them victory, and they forced him and his men to fleed. They killed nine thousand of his men, and the rest were dispersed. Judas and his troops returned to Nicanor's camp, and plundered it, seizing a great deal of property from the merchants, which they divided among the injured.

This battle took place on the sixth day of the week, so Judas and his men remained there until the sabbath day had passed. Then they marched against Ptolemy and Gorgias, whom they found and defeated, and in their victory slaughtered twenty thousand of their troops. Ptolemy and Gorgias fled, and Judas and his militia pursued them but could not capture them, because they took shelter in a city of two idols, and fortified themselves within it with the remnant of their army.

Judas attacked Philip, and he fled from before him. Judas pursued him, and he entered into a nearby house and locked the doors, as it was a fortified house. Judas commanded it was set on fire, and the house was burned, with Philip in it. So Judas took vengeance on him for Eleazar and the others whom Philip had put to death. Afterward, they returned to the dead soldiers and pillaged their armor, but the best of the plunder they sent into the Holy Land.[1]

Nicanor disguised himself and sneaked away. He returned to Lysias and told him what had happened to him and his army.

Chapter 7 Notes

1 Arabic: ālôrd ālmqdsà (أَلأَرْض أَلْمُقَدَّسَة). Translation: the land that is sacred

The Arabic term is likely a translation of the Palestinean Aramaic term àrṣ mqdšà (ארץ מקדשא), meaning 'land (or place) of the sanctuary (or temple).' The term was adopted into many languages via Greek, Latin, and Arabic, and is commonly translated as 'holy land,' in many languages. In this verse, it appears to be a specific reference to the land around Jerusalem which they had control over.

Chapter 8

Antiochus returned quickly from Parthia with his army disbanded. When he had learned what had happened to his army which Lysias had sent out, and to all his men, he gathered a large army and marched to the land of Judea. As he marched, near the middle of his journey, God attacked his troops with almighty weapons, but this could not stop him from his march. He persisted, uttering all sorts of insolence against God, and saying that no one could turn him aside, nor slow him from his determined purposes. Therefore the great and good God infected him also with ulcers, which attacked the whole of his body, but even still he did not stop, nor turn back from his journey, and was even more filled with wrath, and inflamed with an eager desire to complete his desire, and to put his plans into effect.

There were many elephants in his army, and one of these got loose and trumpeted, which frightened the horses that were pulling the carriage that Antiochus was lying in. The horses ran off, and he fell out, and as he was fat and corpulent, his limbs were bruised, and some of his joints were dislocated. The bad smell of his ulcers, which already sent out a rotten odor, became worse, so neither he nor those who approached him could endure it. When he fell, his servants picked him up and carried him upon their shoulders, but as the smell grew worse, they put him down and retreated a distance from him.

CHAPTER 8

Seeing the evils which surrounded him, he believed that it was a punishment that had come upon him from the great and good God, because of the injustice and the tyranny which he had exercised towards the Hebrew men,[1] and the pointless shedding of their blood. Fearfully, he turned himself to God, and, confessing his sins, said, "Oh God, in truth I deserve the things which You have sent upon me, and You are just in your judgments. You humblest he who is exalted, and bringest down he who is arrogant. Your is greatness, and magnificence, and majesty, and prowess. Truly, I have oppressed the people, and have both acted and decreed tyrannically against them. Forgive, I beg You oh God, this, my error, and wipe out my sin, and return to me my health, and I will fill the treasury of your house with gold and silver, and cover the floor of the house of your sanctuary with purple carpet, and be circumcised, and to proclaim throughout all my kingdom, that You only are the true God, without any partner, and that there is no God besides you."

But God did not hear his prayers, nor accept his supplication. His troubles were increased on him, and he lost control of his bowels. His ulcers increased to the degree that his flesh dropped off his body. Then he died and was buried. In his place his son reigned, whose name was Eupator.[2]

Chapter 8 Notes

1 Arabic: ôbrānywn (عِبْرَانِيُّونَ). Translation: Hebrew men

2 Arabic: ôfātwr (إفاتور). Translation: Eupator

Antiochus V Eupator (Αντίοχος Ε' Ευπάτωρ) was the heir to Antiochus IV Epiphanes, who is believed to have nominally ruled the Seleucid Empire between 164 and 161 BC. Eupator was nine when his father died in Parthia, and General Lysias was the regent of the empire during his brief reign. There are no Greek records of Epiphanes returning to Judea. All historical records report he died in Isfahan, Iran, after defeating the Parthians and Armenians. The Septuagint's 2ⁿᵈ Maccabees reports that he died after the priests of the temple of Nanaya (Ναναιας) stoned him for desecrating her temple, and there are some corroborating stories from Mesopotamia that support the idea that the goddess herself killed him. The goddess in question was likely the Armenian version: Nane (Նանէ), as this desecration took place in Armenia. Nane was the Armenian version of the Aramaic name Nny (𐡍𐡍𐡉), itself a translation of the Mesopotamian name ᵈᵉⁱᵗʸNanaa (𒀭𒈾𒈾), more commonly called Nanaya today.

Nanaya was a minor Sumerian love goddess who was worshiped until the 5ᵗʰ century AD by various Mesopotamian cultures. It's unclear where the story of the elephant came from, however, rogue elephant stories are common from the military campaigns of the era. As it is unclear what caused Epiphanes' sudden death, it is possible that he was involved in an incident with a rogue elephant, which led to his death.

61

Chapter 9

After Judas had caused Ptolemy, Nicanor, and Gorgias to flee, and had slain their men, he and his soldiers returned to the country of the sacred temple. He commanded all the altars to be destroyed which Antiochus had ordered to be built, and he removed all the idols which were in the sanctuary. Then they built a new altar, and he commanded sacrifices to be offered on in.

They prayed also to the great and good God, that He would bring out the holy fire which would remain upon the altar, and fire came out from some stones of the altar, and burned up the wood and the sacrifices. From it, a fire continued on the altar until the third diaspora. Then they kept the festival of the new altar for eight days, beginning on the twenty-fifth day of the month Kislev. Then they placed bread on the altar of the temple of God and lit the lamps. On each of these eight days, they assembled for prayer and praise, and also they appointed it an ordinance for every year to follow.

Chapter 10

After the days of dedication, Judas marched into the country of the Edomites, to Mount Sier[1] as Gorgias was staying there. Gorgias went out against him with a great army, and there were many battles between them, and there fell of Gorgias' men twenty thousand. Gorgias fled to Acre[2] in the land to the west, as Antiochus had made him governor of that land, and he was residing there, and he told him what had happened.

Then Ptolemy went out with an army of a hundred and twenty thousand men from Macedonia and the east. He went on until he came to the land of Giares (which is Gilead and the adjacent regions), and he slaughtered great numbers of the Judahites. So they wrote to Judas, telling him what had happened to them, begging him to come and defeat Ptolemy and drive him away. Their letter reached him at the same time that a similar letter came to him from the inhabitants of the mountains of Galilee informing him how the Macedonians who were at Tyre and Sidon had now united against them and had attacked them, killing several.

Once Judas had read both letters, he called together his men and showed them the contents of the letters, and appointed a fast and a supplication. After this, he ordered his brother Simeon to take three thousand Judahites, to march as rapidly as possible to the mountains of Galilee, and to suppress the Macedonians who were there, and so Simeon went, while Judas marched to engage Ptolemy. Simeon attacked the Macedonians unexpectedly, and slaughtered eight thousand men, bringing peace to the Galilaeans.

Judas marched until he approached Gorgias and Ptolemy, then attacked them, and the two armies engaged, and very fierce battles took place between them.

Ptolemy headed numerous strong and brave men, and Judas was accompanied by a very small militia, yet, as the people who were with him consisted of the bravest and strongest soldiers, he steadily resisted, and the battle between them lasted long, and grew very bitter. Then Judas called out to the great and good God and invoked his aid, and he said that he had seen five particular young cavalrymen, three of whom fought against Ptolemy's army, and two remained near him. When he watched them attentively, they seemed to him to be messengers from God. Then his heart was comforted, and the hearts of his companions, and after multiple attacks against the enemy, they put them to flight and slaughtered a great multitude of them. The number of those who were killed in Ptolemy's army, from the beginning of this battle until the end, was twenty thousand and five hundred.

CHAPTER 10

After this, Ptolemy and his men fled to the coast, while Judas pursued them and slaughtered as many of them as he caught. Ptolemy fled to Gaza and remained there, and the men of Chalisam came to him. Judas marched against them, and when he found them, he defeated them. Ptolemy's men were dispersed, but he himself fled to Gaza, and there fortified himself. Judas' men pursued the fleeing soldiers and slaughtered a great number of them.

Judas and the men who were with him marched straight to Gaza, and he pitched his camp and besieged it. Judas' men returned to him, and those who were left of Ptolemy's forces retreated into the fortification and insulted Judas.

The arguing between them and Judas' soldiers lasted for five days, however, on the fifth day, as the people continued to insult Judas, and to revile his religion, twenty of Judas' men grew angry. They took shields in their left hands, and swords in their right, and led a man carrying a ladder they had made. They approached the wall, and eighteen of them stood shooting arrows at those who were on the wall, while two ran to the wall, raised the ladder, and climbed up onto the wall. Some of those who were there, seeing that they had ascended and that their comrades were following, retreated from the wall into the city.

CHAPTER 10

Judas' men followed them down from the wall, and defeated them, slaughtering a great number of their enemies. The army of Judas pressed forward to the gate of the city, and the twenty inside charged at the gate attempting to open it, but they were fiercely driven back. They called out loudly so Judas knew his men were near the gate, and the battle grew worse both outside the gate and inside. Judas and his men attacked the gate with fire, and it collapsed, but the men inside died.

The men who had insulted Judas were captured, and he commanded them to be brought out and burned. Moreover, he commanded the city to be utterly slaughtered with the sword. The slaughter continued for two days, and then it was destroyed by fire.

However, Ptolemy had fled, and there were no reports of him heard at that time. He had changed his clothes and hidden himself in one of the pits, and so nothing was known of him at the time. His two brothers were captured and brought to Judas, and he ordered them to be beheaded. After this, he returned to the land of the temple with a great deal of plunder, and both he and his company offered prayers there, giving thanks to God for the benefits which they had received.

Chapter 10 Notes

1 Arabic: ğbāl ālšrāȧ (جبال الشراة). Translation: Mount Seir

This is the Arabic name of Mount Seir, in southwest Jordan. At the time, the Nabatean capital was the nearby city of Petra, and this is likely where Gorgias retreated. Today, the entire region is known by the name ğbāl ālšrāȧ (جبال الشراة), and it is possible the Nabatean Arabs did as well.

2 Arabic: bṭlymws (بطليموس). Translation: Ptolemais (or Acre)

Ptolemais (Πτολεμαΐς) was the Greek name of Acre, in modern northern Israel, during their rule of the region.

Chapter 11

The name of the previously mentioned Antiochus was Epiphanius, but the name of his son who reigned after him was Eupator, who also was named Antiochus. After the battles of Judas with these generals had taken place, they wrote about it to Eupator, who sent with Lysias, his cousin's son, a large army, in which were eighty thousand cavalry and eighty elephants. They marched to the city of Beth-Zur,[1] pitched their camp around it, and laid siege to it, because it was a large city, and many people were there. Lysias raised engines of war around it and began to besiege the inhabitants.

When Judas heard, he and his militia went out to some fortified mountains, and remained there, as if they remained in any city, Lysias could come and besiege it, and overpower them. Judas collected his militia and decided to march them to Lysias' camp, after they went to the temple of God and offered sacrifices in it, praying the great and good God would turn away the malice of their enemies towards them, and grant them victory. After doing this, they marched from the region of the holy house to Beth-Zur, as they had planned to attack the army suddenly, and to defeat it without a struggle.

Men report, that Judas saw someone between the sky and land, riding on a fiery horse, and holding in his hand a large spear, with which he attacked the army of the

Gentiles. What they had seen gave them additional courage and spirits, and they rushed and charged the army, and slaughtered a great number of them. Then the enemy's army was troubled and thrown into complete confusion, and all of them suddenly fled in confusion. The sword of Judas and his militia pressed fiercely against them, and he slaughtered eleven thousand infantrymen and sixteen hundred cavalrymen. Lysias and his guards were also chased to a distant place, where he found safety.

He sent an offer to Judas, asking him to be subject to the king, while his people retained their own religion. Judas agreed provisionally to this until word could be written to the king, and a reply confirming his agreement was received. Judas wrote regarding this, and Lysias also wrote to the king, informing him of what had happened, and what proof he had of the strength and bravery of the Judean people, and that continuing the war with them would exterminate his men like the previous men had been slaughtered. He told him also of their agreement, and that he was waiting to receive a letter providing further commands.

The king replied that it seemed right for him to make peace with the Judean people, removing disagreement regarding their religion, for that this very thing had incited them to the revolts, and the attacks made on his predecessor. He also commanded to make a treaty of peace and obedience with them, so that no obstacles should be placed in their way regarding religion. He also wrote to Judas, and to all the Judeans who were in the land of Judea, explaining this agreement, and this peace continued between them for some time.

Chapter 11 Notes

1 Arabic: byt tr (بیت تر)

This is generally accepted as an alternate spelling of byt zwr (بیت زور), the name of an ancient town in the West Bank south of Jerusalem. It was called Byt Ṣwr (בית צור) in Masoretic *Divrei-hayyamim*, and Betsoura (Βετσουρα) in the Septuagint's *Paralipomena*. The Arabic name used in this book is a direct transliteration of the name used in Hebrew Maccabees: Byt Tr (בית תר), indicating that the author of Arabic Maccabees used Hebrew Maccabees as a source. Tr (תר) is almost certainly a Hebrew transliteration of the Aramaic word twr (קטור), as both twr and ṣwr, mean 'rock,' or 'flint.' Hebrew Maccabees appear to have been translated from an older Aramaic text into Hebrew for the Iberian Jews, as the Iberian Jews never adopted Aramaic. The name is normalized to Beth-Zur in this translation.

Chapter 12

During this era, the prestige of the Romans grew, so the great and good God might fulfill that which Daniel the prophet (peace be upon him,)[1] had prophesied regarding the fourth empire.

There was also at this time a certain most liberal king of Africa,[2] whose name was Hannibal.[3] The royal seat of his empire was Carthage, and he decided to conquer the Roman kingdom, so they united against him. There were many wars between them, and they fought eighteen battles in ten years, yet they were not able to drive him out of their country because of his innumerable army and people. They decided to raise a large force of their bravest soldiers, and attack Hannibal, and continue until they turned his forces back, which they ultimately did. They placed at the head of their armies two most renowned men: Aemilius[4] and Varro.[5]

They met Hannibal and engaged his army, and ninety thousand[6] men from their army were killed, and forty thousand of Hannibal's army were killed. Aemilius also was killed in that battle, but Varro fled to a large fortified city called Venusia. Hannibal did not pursue him, but he marched to Rome, to capture it permanently. He laid siege to it for eight days and began to build fortifications around it. When the citizens saw this, they decided to enter into a peace treaty with him, even if this included surrendering the country.

There was a young man among them named Scipio.[7] At the time the Romans were without a king, and the entire administration of their government was conducted by three hundred and twenty men, over whom presided a senior or elder. Scipio went to these and persuaded them not to trust Hannibal nor to surrender to him. They answered that they did not trust him, but that they were unable to resist him.

He replied to them, "The whole land of Africa is completely empty of soldiers because they are all with Hannibal. Therefore, give me a regiment of the best men, and I will go to Africa. I will perform great feats there, and when news of them reaches him, he will leave you. You will be freed from him and will be in peace. Given time to strengthen your resources, if he should return, you will be able to defend against him"

Scipio's proposal seemed right to them, so they committed thirty thousand of their bravest men to him, and he proceeded to Africa. And Hasdrubal[8] the brother of Hannibal met him, and fought with him, however Scipio defeated him. Then he cut off his head,[9] and took it, with the rest of the bounty back to Rome. He mounted the rampart, and called to Hannibal, saying,

"How will you be able to defeat our country, when you cannot expel me from your own land, where I have gone! I have destroyed it! I have killed your brother, and brought back his head!"

Then he threw the head to him. It was taken to Hannibal and he recognized it. He was infuriated against the people and swore that he would not leave until he had captured Rome. The citizens decided, in order to lure him away, to send Scipio back to besiege and attack Carthage. Scipio returned with his army to Africa, and they pitched their camp around Carthage and besieged it with a most active siege. The inhabitants wrote to Hannibal, saying, "You desire a foreign country, which you do not know if you will be able to win or not, yet one comes into your own country who is endeavoring to conquer it. If you delay returning, we will surrender the country to him, and will give up your family and all your property and your treasures, so we and our property may go unmolested."

When this letter was brought to him, he left Rome and rushed back to Africa, and Scipio went out and met him, and fought a most fierce battle with him three times, in which fifty thousand of his men died. Hannibal was put to flight and retreated to the land of Egypt. Scipio pursued him, captured him, and returned to

CHAPTER 12

Africa. Once he was there, Hannibal was afraid to be seen by the Africans. so he took poison and died.[10]

Scipio defeated the country of Africa and took possession of all the goods, servants, and treasures of Hannibal for himself. Through this, the fame of the Romans was magnified, and their power from that time began to increase.

Chapter 12 Notes

1 Arabic: ôlyh l-lslm (عَلَيْهِ ٱلسَّلَٰمُ). Translation: peace be upon him

'Peace be upon him,' is an Islamic honorific for the dead prophets, which indicates the Arabic text was likely copied by a Muslim scribe at some point. The interpretation of Daniel's fourth kingdom is Roman-era, supporting the original compilation of Maccabees materials being made in that era.

2 Arabic: ôfryqyā (أَفْرِيقِيَا). Translation: Africa

This chapter is about the Roman conquest of Carthage, which became the Roman province of Africa, named after the Ifri people who lived there. The word ifri (ⵉⴼⵔⵉ) is Amazigh (Berber) for 'cave,' and most of the indigenous settlements in the region were built underground. The term 'Africa' was not applied to the entire continent until a few hundred years ago, and so the Africa in the text would have been a reference to the Roman province.

3 Arabic: ḥnbôl (حنبعل). Translation: Hannibal

Hannibal (𐤇𐤍𐤁𐤏𐤋) was a general and statesman, but not a king.

4 Arabic: ômylyws (أميليوس). Translation: Aemilius

Lucius Aemilius Paullus was elected consul of the Roman Republic in 219 BC. He died in combat against Hannibal's forces in the Battle of Cannae that year. This was during the Second Punic War.

5 Arabic: fārw (فارو). Translation: Varro

Gaius Terentius Varro was elected consul in 216 BC and was co-commander of the Roman forces at the Battle of Cannae, where Consul Lucius Aemilius Paullus died. The Romans elected their military commanders, and Varro, as the son of a butcher, was not the best person to lead an army. Over 40,000 Romans died on the first day of the engagement, including Aemilius, and Varro fled to the fortified city of Venusia with 4,500 troops. He later heard that a larger number of Roman survivors from the battle had amassed as Canusium, which he marched to and took command of, forming an army of around 40,000, less than half of the original size of the army that he and Aemilius had commanded.

6 The combined armies under the command of Varro and Aemilius amounted to 85,000, and somewhere between 40,000 and 45,000 were killed in the Battle of Cannae by Hannibal's forces.

7 Arabic: šybywn (شيبيون). Translation: Scipio

Publius Cornelius Scipio Africanus was the Roman general and statesman who defeated Hannibal at the Battle of Zama in 202 BC.

CHAPTER 12 NOTES

8 Arabic: ṣdrbôl (صدربعل). Translation: Hasdrubal

Hasdrubal was the Latin spelling of Ôzrubôl (𐤋𐤏𐤆𐤓𐤁𐤋). Hannibal did have a brother known as Ôzrubôl bn Brq (𐤁𐤓𐤒 𐤁𐤍 𐤋𐤏𐤆𐤓𐤁𐤋), however, he died five years before Scipio's invasion of Africa. The initial defense of Carthage was led by Ôzrubôl bn Gŕskn (𐤂𐤓𐤎𐤊𐤍 𐤁𐤍 𐤋𐤏𐤆𐤓𐤁𐤋), known as Hasdrubal Gisco in Latin. He committed suicide shortly after Scipio defeated him.

Hannibal and his other brother Mgw (𐤌𐤂𐤅), known in Latin as Mago, returned from Italy with their armies to defend Carthage. Historians debate what happened to Mago, with most accepting the Roman historian Livy's account, recorded in the 1st century AD, that Mago died at sea before reaching Africa. Conversely, the earlier Roman historian Cornelius Nepos, writing in the 1st century BC, reported that he fought in Africa, and later traveled with Hannibal until the Carthaginian senate arrested him in 193 BC. Nepos reported that after he escaped custody he later died in a shipwreck.

9 Hasdrubal's head was cut off, however, it was by Claudius Nero after the battle of Metaurus, in Italy, in 207 BC. Nero had it packed in a sack and thrown into Hannibal's camp.

10 It is unclear what the author is referring to, and may have simply been writing fiction at this point. Livy reported that 16,000 were killed in the Battle of Zama, but General Hannibal survived. He did not flee to Egypt, or take his own life, but supported the terms of Carthage's surrender before the Carthaginian Senate.

Chapter 13

From the elder and three hundred and twenty governors to Judas, general of the army, and to the Judeans. Health be to you.

We have already heard of your victories, and courage, and endurance in war, for which we rejoice. We understand that you have entered into an agreement with Antiochus. We write to you to this effect, that you should be friends with us, and not with the Greeks who have fought with you. Moreover, we intend to go to Antioch and to make war upon its lands, so quickly let us know who your enemies are, and with whom you have an agreement of friendship, so we may act accordingly.

This is the treaty made by the elder and three hundred and twenty governors with Judas, general of the army, and the Judeans, that they should be allied to the Romans, and that the Romans and Judeans may be of one mind in wars and victories forever. Now, if war should come upon the Romans, Judas and his people would help them, giving no aid to the enemies of the Romans through trade or through any kind of weapons. And when war would come upon the Judeans, the Romans would help them, by giving no aid to their enemies through any kind of assistance. As the Judeans were allied to the Romans, likewise the Romans to the Judeans, without any inequity. Judas and his people accepted this, and the treaty was established and continued between them and the Romans for a long time.

Chapter 14

After this, Ptolemy amassed a hundred and twenty thousand infantry, and a thousand cavalry, and they went after Judas. Judas met him with ten thousand infantry and routed him, and many of Ptolemy's men were killed. He contacted Judas, and humbly asked him to let him escape with his life, and swore that he would never again make war against him and that he would be kind to the Judeans who were in all his countries. Judas had compassion on him, and let him go, and Ptolemy lived by his oath.

Gorgias amassed three thousand infantry from Mount Seir that is in Edom,[1] and four hundred cavalry, and met Judas, and killed the captain of his army and some of his men. Then Judas and his men advanced towards them, and Gorgias retreated. The majority of his army was killed or fled. He was searched for, but no news was heard of him, however, it was said that he fell in the battle.

Chapter 14 Notes

1 There was a smaller place also called 'Mount Seir' near Hebron in the region of the modern West Bank.

Chapter 15

When word was brought to Antiochus Eupator that Judas' forces had gained strength, and what victories he had achieved, he was very angry and broke the treaty he had made with Judas.

He amassed a large army, that included twenty-two war elephants, and he marched with Lysias his cousin's son into the country of Judea, towards the city Beth-Zur, where he pitched his camp and laid siege to it.

When Judas heard about this, he and the Sanhedrin[1] met together, and prayed to the great and good God, offering many sacrifices.

When they were complete, Judas traveled with the leaders of his forces, entered the camp by night, and suddenly attacked them, killing four thousand of the enemy's men and one of the elephants. He returned to his own camp and waited for dawn, then each army marched out, and the battle grew fierce between them. Judas saw one of the elephants with golden armor, and he thought that the king was sitting on it, so he called his men, and asked them, "Which of you will go out and kill that elephant?"

One of his servants, a young man named Eleazar, went out and rushed the enemy's line, attacking to the right and left, so that the men turned to the sides and did not see him. Then he went forward and approached the elephant, crept under it and slashed open its belly. The elephant fell down on top of him, and he died. So the king seeing this, commanded a retreat, and it was done. The number of men of the higher rank killed that day in the battle was eight hundred, besides the common men who were killed and also those who had been killed during the night.

After this, the king was informed that a friend of him named Philip had revolted, and that Demetrius[2] the son of Seleucus had left Rome with a great army of Romans intending to take the kingdom out of his hands. This caused him a great deal of fear, and he sent a message to Judas offering peace between them, which Judas agreed to. Antiochus, and Lysias his cousin's son, swore to him, that they would never again make war against him.

The king sent a large sum of money to Judas as a present to the temple of God. The king also commanded Menelaus to be arrested, one of the three wicked men who had brought evil on the Judeans in the days of Antiochus his father. He ordered him to be carried up to a high tower and to be thrown off, which was done. Through this, the king planned to gratify the Judeans, since this man was one of their main enemies, and had killed large numbers of them.

Chapter 15 Notes

1 The Sanhedrin (συνέδριον / סנהדרין) was a legal council common in Hellenistic countries, somewhat similar to a supreme court. In the case of Judea, there was the great Sanhedrin in Jerusalem, presided over by the high priest and 70 older judges, for a total of 71 members. There were also the lesser Sanhedrins in the other towns, presided over by 23 judges. The Arabic text uses phrases that translate as 'elders of the Israelites,' 'council of elders,' and 'seventy elders,' which are rendered as 'Sanhedrin' in this translation in order to remove ambiguity. The term 'Sanhedrin,' was dropped by the council in 200 AD, in order to avoid persecution from the Roman authorities, and the term 'house of learning' was adopted. This indicates the Palestinian Arabic author lived after 200 AD.

2 Arabic: dymytryws (ديميتريوس). Translation: Demetrius

Demetrius I Soter (Δημήτριος Α` Σωτήρ) was the son of Seleucus IV Philopator, however, he was sent to Rome as a hostage when he was three years old as one of the terms of the Treaty of Apamea that had ended the Roman-Seleucid War. Even though he was the legal heir to the Seleucid Empire, Rome refused to release him when his father died, and his younger brother Antiochus V Eupator became king, with his cousin Lysias as regent. When Seleucus IV died, and again two years later, Demetrius petitioned Rome to release him so he could take his throne, however, Rome refused. After the second refusal, Demetrius escaped from Rome and made his way to the Seleucid capital city of Antioch, where he rallied the nobles against Antiochus V and Lysias. After they were captured, he had them both executed.

Chapter 16

After this, King Eupator marched into the country of Macedonia, and then returned to Antioch, which Demetrius had attacked with an army of Romans, and defeated. He had killed Lysias his cousin's son, and he reigned at Antioch.

Alcimus, the leader of those three wicked men, who entered his presence, prostrated himself and wept vehemently, saying, "Oh king, Judas and his militia have been murdering great numbers of us because we have deserted their religion, and have accepted the religion of the king. Therefore, oh king, assist us against them, and avenge us on them."

Then he called the Judeans to him, and incensed him, suggesting things to provoke Demetrius and irritate enough him to outfit an army to defeat Judas.

The king listened to them and sent General Nicanor with a great army and a large supply of weapons of war. When Nicanor had entered the sacred land, he sent messengers to Judas asking to meet him, but he did not tell him that he had come to conquer the people but stated that he only came because of the peace which was made between him and the people and that they also were under obedience to the Romans. Judas went to meet him with some of his men, who were the strongest and most courageous, and he commanded them not to go far from him, in case Demetrius might attack him.

When he met Demetrius, he saluted him, and they each sat on the seat that had been prepared for them. Demetrius spoke with him as he pleased, and afterward, each of them went into a tent that the soldiers had erected for him. Nicanor and Judas traveled into the sacred city, and both lived there, and a close friendship grew between them.

When Alcimus found out, he went to Demetrius and incensed him against Judas again. He persuaded him to write a command to Nicanor to send Judas to him bound in chains. Reports of this reached Judas, and he sneaked out of the city at night and traveled to Samaria,[1] and sent for his companions to join him. Once they had arrived, he sounded the trumpet and commanded them to prepare to attack Nicanor.

Nicanor searched for Judas with great diligence, yet could learn nothing of his location. He went to the temple of God, asking the priests to tell him his location so he could send him bound in chains to the king, but they swore that he had not come into the temple of God. Because of this, he abused both them and the temple of God. He insulted the temple and threatened to demolish it from its very foundations, and then left in a rage.

He also searched all the houses in the sacred city thoroughly. He sent his men to the house of a famous man, who had been arrested in the time of Antiochus, and tortured badly, but after the death of Antiochus, the Judeans gave him authority and greatly honored him. When the messengers of Nicanor came to him, he was afraid it would be like it had been in the time of Antiochus, and so he killed himself. When Judas found out, he was very sorry and grieved, and he sent word to Nicanor, saying, "Do not look for me in the city, as I am not there. Come out to me, so we can meet each other, either on the plains or in the mountains. You choose."

Nicanor went out to him, and Judas prepared to meet him with these words, "O God, it was You who exterminated the army of King Sennacherib, and he was greater than this man, in fame, in empire, and in the numbers of his army. You saved King Hezekiah of Judah from him when he had trusted in You and prayed to You, 'Save us, I beg you, Oh God, from his malice and make us victorious over him.'"

Then he prepared himself for battle, and met with Nicanor, and said, "Prepare yourself, I'm coming for you."

Nicanor turned his back to leave, and Judas jumped up and struck him between the shoulders, which he cleaved apart, and his men fled in disarray. Thirty thousand of them fell on that day. The inhabitants of the cities went out and attacked them so that not one of them was left alive. They decreed that that day should be a day of thanksgiving to the great and good God every year, and a day of joy, feasting, and drinking.

Chapter 16 Notes

1 Arabic: sbsṭyå (سبسطية). Translation: Sebastia

Sebasti (Σεβαστη) was the Greek name of the village the Samaritans called Šōmrōn (𐤔𐤌𐤓𐤍). The name was not adopted until the era of Herod the Great, almost a century after the events, so any earlier record would have probably called the village the older Greek name of Samaria (Σαμάρεια). The village had once been the capital of the kingdom of Isreal, and later the capital of the Neo-Assyrian district of Samaria (𒆳𒊓𒈨𒊑𒈾), however, was a minor village by the time of Judas.

Chapter 17

When it was nearly the same time of the year again, Bacchides went out with thirty thousand of the bravest of the Macedonians and marched against Judas without him hearing any reports of their approach, while he was in a city called Lalis, with three thousand men.

Most of those who were with him fled, and only eight hundred men remained with him, including his brothers Simeon and Jonathan. Those who remained with Judas were the strongest and bravest, and who had already survived much in the wars that he had fought. Judas and his militia went out to meet Bacchides and his army.

Bacchides divided his army, placing fifteen thousand to the right of Judas and his militia, and fifteen thousand to their left. Then each division shouted against Judas and his militia. When they carefully examined each, they saw that the enemy's strongest and bravest troops were on the right, and saw that Bacchides himself was among them. Judas likewise divided his company and took the bravest of them with him, and gave the rest to his brothers.

Then he charged to the right, and his militia slaughtered about two thousand men. When he saw Bacchides, he ran towards him and slaughtered all the bravest men who were around him. He and his militia fought off the multitudes that pressed in around them, knocking to the ground the majority of them. Then he approached Bacchides. When Bacchides saw him stalking him like a lion, wielding a great sword in his hands dripping with blood, he was terrified of him, and trembled, and fled out of his sight. Judas and his militia pursued him, and they slaughtered his people with the sword, killing more than half of those fifteen thousand. Bacchides fled to Ashdod.

The fifteen thousand on Judas' left, flanked him and attacked Judas, who by this time had become greatly fatigued, along with his brothers and the rest with them. Those fifteen thousand charged them, and a great battle took place between them and Judas, and many fell on both sides, including Judas.

His brothers carried him away and buried him beside the sepulcher of Mattathias his father (God be merciful to them), and the Israelites mourned many days for him. He had governed for seven years, and Jonathan his brother succeeded him in the government.

Chapter 18

Jonathan succeeded his brother, and he went to the Jordan with a small number of men. When Bacchides heard of it, he marched to him with a large army. When Jonathan saw him, his men swam across the Jordan, and Bacchides and his army followed them and surrounded them. Jonathan rushed at Bacchides, and as the men gave way to Jonathan, he and his militia left from the middle of them and traveled to Beersheba.

His brother Simeon joined him, and they lived there. They repaired the fortifications that had fallen down and fortified themselves there.

Bacchides marched to them and besieged them, and Jonathan and his brother, and those who were with them, went out to him at night and killed great numbers of his army, and burned the battering rams and engines of war. His army was dispersed and Bacchides fled into the desert.

Jonathan and Simeon, and the men who were with him, pursued and captured him. When he saw Jonathan, he knew that his death was near, so he proclaimed peace with Jonathan, and swore that he would never again make war against him, and also that he would release all of the slaves which he had taken from the army of Judas.

Jonathan shook his hand, and departed from him, and there were no more wars between them after this. Not

CHAPTER 18

long after this, Jonathan died, and his brother Simeon
succeeded him.

Chapter 19

Simeon the son of Mattathias succeeded to the government, and he gathered together all those who remained of the militia of Judas. His affairs prospered, and he conquered all those who had been hostile towards the Judeans after the death of his brother Judas. He treated his people well, and intelligently managed his country.

As a result, Antiochus attacked him, and also Demetrius the son of Seleucus, sent a great army against him. Simeon and his two sons went out to meet them, and he divided his army into two parts, one he kept with himself, and the other he gave to his sons. Then he and those who were with him approached the army, while he sent his two sons and their militia by another route, and ordered them to attack the army at a given time.

He found the army of Antiochus and attacked it, and began to prevail against it. His two sons arrived when the battle had already begun, and the fighting grew fierce. They came around the rear of the army, and Antiochus' army, now between two armies, was cut to pieces. Not a single man of them escaped, nor did Antiochus return again to fight with Simeon.

Peace and calm continued among the Judeans all the days of Simeon, and the time of his government was two years. Then Ptolemy his son-in-law attacked him and killed him when he was present at a feast. He also seized his wife and his two sons. Simeon's son, whose name was Hyrcanus, was set in his father's position.

Chapter 20

While Simeon was still alive, he had appointed his son John to be captain, and after gathering a great many soldiers for him, he sent him to vanquish a man who had come out against him, called Hyrcanus. He was a man of great fame, powerful and strong, and descended from an ancient king. Jonathan encountered and defeated him, and so Simeon named his son John Hyrcanus, because of his killing Hyrcanus, and being victorious over him.

When Hyrcanus heard that Ptolemy had killed his father, he was afraid of Ptolemy and fled to Gaza. Ptolemy pursued him with a great force, but the citizens of Gaza helped Hyrcanus, and barred the gates of their city, blocking Ptolemy from reaching Hyrcanus. Ptolemy returned, and departed to Dagon, having with him the mother of Hyrcanus and his two brothers. At the time, Dagon was a strongly fortified castle.

Hyrcanus went to the sacred temple to offer sacrifices and pray to succeed his father. He amassed a large militia and went to attack Ptolemy. Ptolemy locked the gate of Dagon with himself and his force inside and fortified himself in there. Hyrcanus besieged him and made an iron ram to batter the wall, and to break it open. The battle between them was long, but Hyrcanus prevailed against Ptolemy, and got close to the castle, and almost captured it.

CHAPTER 20

When Ptolemy saw this, he commanded the mother of Hyrcanus and his two brothers to be brought up on the wall and to be tortured severely, which was done to them. Hyrcanus, seeing this, held back, afraid they would be killed and withdrew from fighting.

Then his mother called out, "My son, do not be moved by love and filial duty towards me and your brother, in preference to your father. Don't be weakened in your desire to avenge him because of our captivity! Demand satisfaction for the rights of your father to your utmost power. What you fear for us from this tyrant, he will certainly do to us in any event, so continue your siege without any break."

When Hyrcanus heard the words of his mother, he continued the siege. Ptolemy increased the torture of his mother and his brothers and swore that he would throw them from the castle, whenever Hyrcanus approached the wall. Hyrcanus was afraid he would be the cause of their death, and he returned to his camp to continue the siege of Ptolemy. It happened that the feast of Tabernacles was coming, and Hyrcanus went into the city of the sacred temple, so he might be present at the feast and the solemnity and the sacrifices. When Ptolemy knew that he had left for the sacred city, and was delayed there, he seized the mother of Hyrcanus and his brothers and killed them. Then he fled to a place where Hyrcanus could not follow.

Chapter 21

When Antiochus heard that Simeon was dead, he amassed an army and marched to the city of the sacred temple, and he camped around it and besieged it, determined to capture it. However, he could not capture it, due to the height and strength of the walls, and the many warriors who were in it. By God's will he was stopped from capturing it.

He decided to attack the northern side of the city and built a hundred and thirty siege towers outside the wall, and had archers on them to attack anyone who tried to go up on the walls of the city. He ordered men to dig up the ground near the wall until they found the foundation, which was made of wood. They burned it with fire, and a large portion of the wall collapsed.

Hyrcanus' men fought them and prevented them from entering, and then guarded the destroyed portion of the wall. Then Hyrcanus went out with the majority of his militia against the army of Antiochus and brutally defeated them. Antiochus and his men were routed, and pursued by Hyrcanus with his troops until they had driven them away from the city. Then they returned to the towers that Antiochus had built and destroyed them, and remained in the city, and camped around it. Antiochus camped about two farsangs[1] away from the city of the temple of God.

CHAPTER 21

As the feast of Tabernacles approached, Hyrcanus sent ambassadors to him requesting a truce until the solemnity had passed. He agreed to this and sent sacrificial victims, and gold and silver to the temple of God. Hyrcanus commanded the priests to accept what Antiochus had sent, and so they did. When Hyrcanus and the priests saw the reverence of Antiochus towards the temple of God, he sent ambassadors to him offering peace. Antiochus agreed, and he went to Jerusalem to meet with Hyrcanus, and they entered the city together. Hyrcanus made a feast for Antiochus and his princes, and they ate and drank together. He paid him a tribute of three hundred talents of gold, and they made an agreement regarding peace and rendering assistance. Then Antiochus returned to his own country.

It was said that Hyrcanus opened the treasury, which had been established by some kings of the descendants of David (peace be upon him), and he took a great sum of money, and later returned the same amount, and then returned it to its former state of secrecy.[2] He rebuilt and repaired the part of the wall that had collapsed, and provided for the convenience and the advantage of his followers, and treated them well.

Once Antiochus had returned to his own country, he decided to go to war with the king of Parthia, as he had revolted from the time of the first Antiochus, and he sent ambassadors to Hyrcanus, so he should go with him. Hyrcanus went with him and departed for the country of Parthia. An army of the Parthians met them and fought with them, but Antiochus defeated them, some fleeing, and some being executed. Then he remained at the site and erected a magnificent building to be a memorial of his victory in their country. After some time, he traveled forward to meet the Parthian king, and Hyrcanus remained behind, as it was the sabbath before Shavuot. The king of Parthia and Antiochus met, and a great battle took place between them in which Antiochus and most of his army were killed.

When news of this was brought to Hyrcanus, he marched into the land of Syria and besieged Aleppo.[3] The citizens surrendered to him, paying him tribute. Then he left them and returned to the sacred city, and remained there for some days.

Later he traveled to the land of Samaria and fought against Nablus,[4] but the citizens stopped him from entering it. He destroyed the buildings they had on Mount Jezabel, including the temple.

(This was two hundred years after Sanballat the Samaritan had built it.)

He also killed the priests who were in Samaria.

CHAPTER 21

He marched into the land of Edom, to Mount Seir, and they surrendered to him. He commanded that they would be circumcised and adopt the religion of the Torah, and they agreed with him, were circumcised, became Judeans, and continued in this practice until the destruction of the second temple. Hyrcanus went on to all the surrounding nations, and they all submitted to him and entered into treaties of peace and subservience.

He sent ambassadors to the Romans, writing to them about the renewal of the alliance between them. When his ambassadors arrived, the Romans honored them and appointed them a seat of dignity. They considered the business of why the embassy had come and replied with the following letter.

Chapter 21 Notes

1 Arabic: frāsẖ (فَرَاسِخ). Translation: farsangs

The farasaxi (𒆠𒂖𒇷𒆠𒌋) was a Persian unit of measurement, which was adopted into many languages, including the Aramaic prsh (פרסח), Armenian hrasax (հրասախ), and Greek parasangês (παρασάγγης). The Aramaic name was later adopted into Syriac as prshå (ܦܪܣܚܐ), which was then adopted into Arabic as frsẖ (فَرْسَخ), while the Greek name was adopted into Latin as parasanga. Unfortunately, the length of the farsang changed widely between cultures using it, allowing for the '2 furlongs' to be anywhere from 3.5 to 9.5 km (2 to 6 miles) from the city.

2 Other sources report that he looted the tomb of David, which caused problems between him and the general Judean population. He is also reported to have evicted all the civilian inhabitants of Jerusalem before the siege, and looted the surrounding countryside, which left a legacy of distrust between him and the general Judean population.

3 Arabic: ḥlbws (حلبوس)

The Arabic name appears to be a transliteration of the Greek name Chalibôs (Χαλιβώς), an ancient Greek spelling of the name of the city of Aleppo, in northern Syria. The Arabic name is ḥalab (حلب), and so the Arabic translation could not have recognized the name. As the Arabic translator does not appear to have been translated from Greek, but Palestinian Aramaic, it was likely spelled as ḥlbws (חלבוס) in the source text that was used. This indicates the original author of the text used Greek source material for the book. The 1ˢᵗ century Judean historian Josephus' *The Judean War* and *Antiquities of the Judeans* are accepted as the source for some of it, but cannot account for all of it.

4 Arabic: nābls (نَابُلس). Translation: Nablus

Nablus was the capital city of the Samaritans under Greek rule. The Arabic name is derived from the Greek name Neopolis (Νεάπολις), meaning 'new city.' The Samaritan name of the city was Šăkēm (ࠔࠊࠌ).

Chapter 22

From the elder, and his three hundred and twenty senators, to Hyrcanus the king of Judea, health.

Your letter has reached us, and on reading it we celebrated. We have questioned your ambassadors regarding the state of your affairs. We have acknowledged their dignity in science, moral discipline, and the virtues, and we have honored them, and let them sit in the presence of our elder, who has been careful to conduct all their business.

He heard the command that all the cities which Antiochus had captured by force were restored to you and that every obstacle to your religion was removed, and all was voided that Antiochus had decreed against you. He has also heard that all the cities which he had captured are loyal to you.

He has decreed an order by letter to all his provinces, that your ambassadors should be treated with respect and honor. Moreover, he has returned with them an ambassador to you named Cynaeus, bearing this letter, to whom also he has entrusted an embassy, that he might negotiate with you in person.

When this letter from the Romans had reached Hyrcanus, he began to be called a king, formerly being called high priest, and so the royal and sacerdotal duties were united in him. He was the first who was called king among the chiefs of the Judeans in the time of the second temple.

Chapter 23

Hyrcanus marched to Samaria and besieged the Samaritans for a long time until he reduced them so much that they were forced to eat every kind of dead animal. Nevertheless, they bore this patiently, afraid of his sword, and trusting to in Macedonians and Egyptians, who they had requested help from.

In the meantime, the days of the great fast were approaching, for which Hyrcanus had to be present in the sacred temple to offer sacrifices. Therefore he substituted his two sons, Antigonus and Aristobulus, as commanders of the army, leaving them orders to besiege the Samaritans and reduce them to the extreme. He commanded the army to obey his sons and to follow their orders, and then he left for the city of the sacred temple.

Antiochus the Macedonian marched to help the Samaritans, and reports of it reached the two sons of Hyrcanus. They substituted a general to continue the siege of Samaria and went to meet Antiochus, whom they encountered and defeated, before returning to Samaria. Also, Lathyros the son of Queen Cleopatra, came from Egypt to help the Samaritans. When news of this was brought to Hyrcanus, he went to meet him as the solemnity was passed. When he met, they fought fiercely, and many of his soldiers were killed. Lathyros fled and did not return to help the Samaritans again.

CHAPTER 23

King Hyrcanus returned to Samaria and continued the struggle until he captured it with the sword. He slaughtered all of its citizens who were remaining, and utterly destroyed it, pulling down its walls.

Chapter 24

Lathyros the son of Cleopatra, after becoming wealthy and respected by men, revolted from Cleopatra his mother, with the help of some of the powerful men of the kingdom. Cleopatra sent for two Judeans, one named Chelcias, and the other Hananias, and placed them at the head of those leaders in Egypt who remained on her side. She made them both generals of the Egyptian army.

They managed all matters well with the common people and conducted the affairs of the empire with wisdom. Cleopatra sent them to fight with Lathyros. They made war against him and routed him, and his men abandoned him. He fled to Cyprus, and there remained, with a few who still supported him.

Chapter 25

At the time, there were three sects among the Judians. One was called the Pharisees, that is, the 'separated,' or religious. Their rule was to follow everything contained in the law, according to the expositions of their forefathers.

The second was the Sadducees. These were followers of a certain man of the doctors named Sadoc. It was their rule to follow the things found in the text of the law, and of which there was a demonstration in the Torah itself, but not that which did not exist in the text, nor was proved from it.

The third sect was that of the Hasideans[1] or those who studied the virtues. (The author of this book did not describe their rules, nor do we know anything of them other than their name, as they applied themselves to practices that were more the eminent virtues, namely, to select from those two other sects whichever was most safe in belief, most sure and guarded.)

Hyrcanus at first was one of the Pharisees. Later he went over to the Sadducees because one of the Pharisees had said to him, "It is not lawful for you to be high priest, because your mother was a slave before she bore you, in the days of Antiochus. The son of a slave cannot be high priest."

CHAPTER 25

This debate took place in the presence of the senior Pharisees, which caused him to go over the rules of the Sadducees. The Sadducees were enemies of the Pharisees, as they constantly disagreed with one another, and they convinced him to murder great numbers of the Pharisees. The problems became so great that conflict and many troubles continued among them for a great length of time.

Chapter 25 Notes

1 Arabic: ḥsydym (حسيديم)

The Arabic word appears to be the direct transliteration of the Hebrew word ḥasiydiym (חֲסִידִים), plural indefinite of ḥasiyd (חָסִיד) meaning the 'pious.' The presence of a direct transliteration of the Hebrew term suggests one of the sources used by the author was written in Hebrew or Palestinian Aramaic.

In the Septuagint's books of the Maccabees the Asidaeoe (Ἀσιδαῖοι) were a sect of Judeans who supported Judas' rebellion. The Vetus Latina book of Esther also claims to be the 'Book of Hadassah, which is called Esther,' indicating it was a holy book of the Hasidean sect. The nature of the sect is debated by scholars, some viewing them as a precursor to the Pharisees, and others viewing them as either a precursor or alternate name of the Essenes (Ἐσσηνοί) sect, who were mentioned by Josephus and others at the time. The Vetus Latin book of Esther is significantly close to both versions of Esther found in Septuagint manuscripts than the abridged version found in the Masoretic texts, suggesting that the Hasideans influenced the development of the Septuagint and Vetus Latina manuscripts.

Chapter 26

Hyrcanus had three sons: Antigonus, Aristobulus, and Alexander. Hyrcanus loved Antigonus and Aristobulus, but he disliked Alexander. At one point, he had a dream in which Alexander reigned after his death, and this distressed him. He did not think it wise while he was still alive to appoint as heir either of the sons that he loved because of his dream, nor to appoint Alexander as king as he disliked him. Therefore, he deferred the decision so that after his death it would be decided according to the will of the great and good God.[1]

In the time of his father and uncles, the Judeans had been united in love towards them, and quick to obey them, because of their conquering their enemies, and the heroic acts they accomplished. They continued united in the love of Hyrcanus until he slaughtered the Pharisees, the inquisition of the Judeans, and the religious civil wars. From then perpetual enmities arose, ceaseless problems, and many murders. Which was the reason why many detested Hyrcanus. He reigned for thirty-one years, and he died.

Chapter 26 Notes

1 This sentence is contrary to other sources, which state he divided the the powers of the state and the church, leaving the crown to his widow, and the high priesthood to his son Judas Aristobulus. Aristobulus rejected this arrangement, and after his father died assumed the kingship. He imprisoned his mother who should have been queen, and reportedly starved her to death. This version of events comes from Josephus, and so the author of Arabic Maccabees must have had a different source for the events.

Chapter 27

When Hyrcanus was dead, his son Aristobulus succeeded him on the throne. He was haughty, prideful, and power-hungry, and placed on a large crown of his head instead of the crown of the sacred priesthood. He loved his brother Antigonus, whom he preferred to all his friends, but his brother Alexander he kept in prison, along with his mother, because of her love for Alexander.[1]

He sent his brother Antigonus to fight against him, and he defeated him and all his co-conspirators and caused his militia to flee. Then he returned to the city of the sacred temple. This happened while Aristobulus was sick in bed. Antigonus heard of his brother's sickness while he was on his way to the city, and after entering the city, he went to the temple of God, to give thanks for the mercy shown in his deliverance from the enemy, and to beg the great and good God to restore health to his brother.

However, some of those who were adversaries of Antigonus went to Aristobulus and said, "The news of your sickness was carried to your brother, and now he is coming with armed partisans. He has gone into the sanctuary to meet his friends, so he may suddenly attack you and kill you."

King Aristobulus was afraid to take any quick action against his brother regarding what had been told to him, as he wanted to know if it was an accurate report. Therefore he commanded his guards to station themselves in a certain place, from which whoever came to his palace could bypass. He likewise ordered a public proclamation, that no one wearing any kind of weapons could come to the king's court, without being invited. After this, he sent to Antigonus, ordering him to come to him, and Antigonus took off his weapons in obedience to the king.

However, a messenger was sent to him from the wife of Aristobulus, who hated him, and said, "The king says to you, 'I have heard of the splendor of your armor when you entered the city, and want to see you dressed in it, so come to me like that, so I may seeing you in your glory.'"

Antigonus did not doubt that this message was from the king, as the messenger had stated, and believed that he did not wish him to be treated like others regarding laying down their arms, so he went to him dressed in his armor. As he traveled past the place where King Aristobulus had stationed his guards with orders to kill anyone who should come past armed, and when the guards saw him wearing his armor, they rushed at him, and quickly killed him. His blood flowed over the marble pavement on that spot, and the cries of men grew loud. They wept and lamentated over the death of Antigonus, for his beauty, and elegance of his discourse, and his exploits.

The king, hearing the mourning of the men, asked about it, and found that Antigonus had been killed. This caused him the greatest sorrow, both because of his love of him, and because he did not deserve this fate. He understood the trap that had been set for his brother, and he cried out loud and wept greatly. He beat his chest constantly until some arteries in his chest burst, and the blood flowed out of his mouth. His attendants and best friends came to him, consoling him, and appeasing and soothing him, to stop him from this action, knowing that he would die, as he was weak, and had almost died from that which he had already done.

They took a golden basin to catch the blood that flowed from his mouth, and they sent an attendant with the basin and blood to a physician, so he might see it and advise what was to be done for him. The attendant was carrying the basin, but when he came to the place where Antigonus had been killed, and his blood had flowed out, the attendant slipped and fell. The king's blood slipped from the basin over the blood of his murdered brother. The attendant returned with the basin and told the courtiers what had happened, who abused and insulted him. He justified himself and swore that he had not intentionally or voluntarily done this. When the king heard them quarreling, he asked what they were saying, but they held their tongues. When he threatened them, they told him, and he said, "Praise be to the Just Judge, who has shed the blood of the oppressor over the blood of the oppressed," then he groaned, and immediately died.

His reign was one full year. And all his supporters mourned him, for he was noble-minded, victorious, and liberal. Then his brother Alexander reigned in his place.

Chapter 27 Notes

1 This is contrary to Josephus' account, which reports that John Hyrcanus left the crown to her, and she was supposed to rule as the queen of Judea.

Chapter 28

After Aristobulus died, his brother Alexander was unshackled from his chains, and released from prison, so he could assume the throne. The governor of the city Acre (which is Ptolemais) had rebelled and had sent messengers to Lathyros the son of Cleopatra, requesting he aid him and protect him. He had refused for a long time, fearing a repeat of what he had previously suffered from Hyrcanus. However, the messenger gave him courage because of the favors promised by the lords of Tyre and Sidon, as well as others. Lathyros marched with thirty thousand men, and the report of it was brought to Alexander, who anticipated him at Ptolemais and attacked it. The citizens of Ptolemais shut the gate in his face and tried to keep him out. However, Alexander confined them, and besieged them, until he heard the Lathyros army was approaching, then he left them as Lathyros and his army were nearby.

Among the citizens of Ptolemais, there was an old man of acknowledged wisdom, who persuaded the citizens not to allow Lathyros to enter their city, or to swear obedience to him, since he was of a different religion. He said to them, "It will be far more advantageous to you in every way to submit to Alexander, who is of the same religion, than submission to Lathyros." He did not stop until they agreed to his viewpoint, and they prevented Lathyros from entering Ptolemais and refused to submit to him. Lathyros' plans were foiled and no one could counsel him on what to do next.

The king of Sidon heard of it, and he sent messengers to him requesting he help him in the war against Alexander, so they could either defeat him outright or at least capture some of his cities to punish him. Then Lathyros could return to his own country, after performing deeds that would make him famous, which would be more advantageous to him than to return without having achieved anything.

Alexander heard of this, and sent to Lathyros an honorable ambassador with a very valuable gift, and requested he not to aid the king of Sidon. Lathyros accepted Alexander's gift and agreed to his request. Then Alexander marched to Sidon and fought against its king. God made him victorious, and he slaughtered great numbers of his men, and after the king fled, took possession of his country.

After this, Alexander sent messengers to Cleopatra, requesting that she should come with an army against Lathyros her son, and offering to march with his army against him and bring him to her in chains. When Lathyros found out, he traveled to the mountains of Galilee, slaughtered many of the inhabitants, and captured ten thousand slaves. Many of his own men also were killed.

From there he marched until he came to the Jordan, where he camped, so his men and horses might have rest, while he prepared to march to Jerusalem to fight with Alexander.

A report of this reached Alexander, who marched against him with fifty thousand men, six thousand of which carried bronze shields, and it was said that each of those could resist many men. He attacked him at the Jordan and fought him there, but was not victorious, because he trusted in the number of his men.

However, with Lathyros some men were very skillful in battles, and in commanding armies, who advised him to divide his forces into two parts, so that one might be with Lathyros while his army prepared for battle, and the other part might be with another captain of their army. He fought until noon, and a great number of his men were killed. His captain marched with the remainder of the army, whose strength was yet full, against Alexander and his men, who were by this time tired, and he had an easy time dispatching them, slaughtering most of them. Alexander and the men who had remained with him fled into the city of the sacred temple.

Lathyros also traveled in the evening into a town nearby, and by chance, some Judean women with their children met him. He commanded some of the children to be killed, and their flesh to be cooked, pretending that some in his army fed on human flesh, intending to strike the fear of his troops into the inhabitants of the country. After this, Cleopatra met with Alexander, and when he told her what Lathyros had done to his army, she appointed him to go with her in search of him. When Lathyros heard, he fled to a port where his ships were docked, boarded one, and returned to Cyprus. Cleopatra returned to Egypt.

At the end of the year, Alexander marched against Gaza, because its chief had revolted from him, and had sent a request to an Arab king named Aretas II[1] to assist him. He agreed to this and marched towards Gaza.

Alexander was informed of this and left some of his men around Gaza, and marched against Aretas II, and attacked him, causing him to flee. Then he returned to Gaza, and beseiging it, captured it at the end of a year. However, he captured it because of the brother of the chief, who suddenly attacked him and killed him. When the citizens wanted to kill him, he collected his friends, went to the gate of the city, and spoke to Alexander, offering that if his life and the lives of his friends was spared, he would allow them to enter the city. Alexander agreed to this, and entered Gaza, and then slaughtered its citizens, and tore down the temple that was in it, and melted the gilded idol which was in the temple.

After this, he returned to the city of the sacred temple, and there celebrated the feast of Tabernacles. When the feast had passed, he prepared for war against Aretas II, whom he later fought, and killed many of his men. Aretas II's affairs were very limited and crippled, and he feared for his own life. Therefore, he surrendered to Alexander in trade for his life, and he offered obedience to him and paid him tributes. Alexander departed from him and marched against Hemath and Tyre, and captured them. Having received tribute from the inhabitants, he returned to the city of the sacred temple.

Chapter 28 Notes

1 Arabic: ḥārṯás (حارثةس)

Ḥrtt II (𐢛𐢛𐢛) was the king of Nabataea between 103 and 96 BC. The Greek transliteration of his name was Arétās (Ἀρέτας), which the Arabic name used here is transliterated from. The modern Arabic name is ḥārṯá (حارثة). The modern English name, Aretas, is derived from the Greek name.

Chapter 29

Afterward, problems arose between the Pharisees and Sadducees and continued for six years. Alexander helped the Sadducees against the Pharisees, of which fifty thousand were killed over six years. Between these two sects, the state of things deteriorated to total warfare, and their enmity was completely confirmed. Alexander sent for the leader of each sect, spoke kindly to them, and advised a reconciliation. But they answered him, "Honestly, in our opinion, you are worthy of death, for the vasteness of innocent blood which you have shed. Therefore let there be nothing between us but the sword."

Then after this, they began to show their enmity openly, sending messengers to Demetrius the king of Macedon, that he should come to them with an army, and promising that they would assist him against Alexander and his allies, and would reduce the Hebrews to submission to the Macedonians. So Demetrius marched to them with a large army.

Alexander was told of this and sent someone to hire six thousand Macedonians who were attached to his own forces as he advanced against Demetrius. Many also of the Pharisee Judeans joined with Demetrius. Demetrius secretly sent people to the Macedonians who were with Alexander, to hire them from him, but they would not hear them. Alexander also secretly sent men to the Judeans who were with Demetrius, to convert them to his side, but these men would have nothing to do with him.

Alexander and Demetrius met and fought a battle, in which all of Alexander's men fell, and he escaped alone back into the land of Judea. When his supporters heard it whispered that he had escaped in safety, and found out where he was, around six thousand of the bravest of the bravest Israelites, and many of those who had revolted against Demetrius, joined him. Afterward, men flocked to him from everywhere, and he returned to battle to Demetrius with a numerous force, and caused him to flee, and Demetrius returned into his own country. Alexander marched against him in Antioch and besieged it for three years. When Demetrius came out to fight, Alexander defeated him and killed him. He departed the city and returned to Jerusalem to his citizens, who glorified him, honoring and praising him for having defeated his enemies. The Judeans agreed to submit to him, and his heart was at peace.

He sent his armies against all his enemies, whom he put to flight, and gained victory over them. He also gained possession of the mountains of Seir, the lands of Ammon, Moab, the Palestinians, and all the parts which were in the hands of the Arabians who fought with him, even to the edge of the desert. And the affairs of his kingdom were ruled correctly, and he placed his people and his country in a state of safety.

Chapter 30

Afterward, King Alexander fell sick with a malarial fever, for three whole years. When the governor of a city named Al-Rajib[1] revolted from him, he led a powerful army there, taking with him his wife and family, and besieged the city.

But when he was on the point of being captured, his disease increased, and his strength declined. His wife, who was named Alexandra, lost all hope of his recovery. She approached him and said, "You know how great your conflict is with the Pharisees. Your two sons are little boys, and I am a woman. Altogether we will not be able to resist them. What advice do you give to me and them?"

He answered her, "My advice is, that you persevere against the city until it is captured, which will be shortly. When it has been defeated, establish its government similar to the other cities. But regarding all these people, pretend that I am sick. Whatever you choose, pretend that you do it at my command. Reveal my death only to those servants whom you trust. When you have finished these matters, go into the city of the sacred temple, with my dried and embalmed body, and fill the place where I lie with perfume so that no unpleasant smell may come from me. When the affairs of the country are settled, go there, and cover me in perfumes, and carry me into the palace, as if I was sick. When I am there, send for the leaders of the Pharisees, and when they come, honor them, and speak nicely with them. Then say, 'Alexander has already died, and see I give him over to you, so do whatever seems good to you. I will from now on follow your directives.' If you do this, I know that they will do nothing to me or you, except that which is good. The people will follow them, and your affairs will be well organized after my death. You will reign securely until your two sons are grown up."

After this, Alexander died, and his wife hid his death. When the city was captured, she returned to Jerusalem and sent for the leaders of the Pharisees. She spoke with them as Alexander had advised her. They replied that Alexander had been their king, and they had been his people, and they spoke to her with affection, and promised to place her at the head of their government. Then they went out and collected men. They took Alexander's body and carried it out magnificently to its burial. They sent for men to appoint Alexandra as queen, and she was appointed. Alexander's reign was twenty-seven years long.

Chapter 30 Notes

1 Arabic: rǧyb (رجيب). Translation: Rajib

The town of āl-Rqym (الرقيم) is located near Amman in modern Jordan. When the Greeks administrated the region it was known as Ragaba (Ραγαβα), which is transliterated into Arabic in this verse, supporting a Greek source text for this chapter. The common English name of the town is Al-Rajib, which is used in this translation.

Chapter 31

While Alexandra reigned, she summoned to her the leaders of the Pharisees and commanded them to write to all those of their sect who had fled into Egypt and other places in the days of Hyrcanus and Alexander, that they could return to the land of Judea. She showed her favor towards them and did not oppose their rites, or forbid their ceremonies, as Alexander and Hyrcanus had forbidden them. She also released all of them who were in prison. They came together from every quarter and the Sadducees she forbade from offering them any violence. Their affairs were well organized, and their condition improved from the end of the conflict.

When Hyrcanus and Aristobulus, the two sons of Alexander, grew up, the queen made Hyrcanus the high priest, as he was meek, mild, and honest. Aristobulus she made general of the army, as he was stout, brave, and jovial. She also gave him the army of the Sadducees, but she did not think it appropriate to appoint him king, as he was still young. She also sent messages to all those who paid tribute to Alexander, and took their kings' sons, whom she kept near her as hostages; and they continued in their obedience to her, paying tribute every year. She walked uprightly with her people, distributing justice, and commanding her people to do the same. Therefore, there was a lasting peace between the parties, and she gained their respect.

Chapter 32

There was among the Sadducees a leader, who had been promoted by Alexander, named Diogenes, who had once convinced him to kill eight hundred Pharisees. The leaders of the Pharisees went to Alexandra and remind her of what Diogenes had done, asking her permission to execute him, which she granted.

Once they received it, they killed many Sadducees along with him, which made the Sadducees very angry. They went to Aristobulus, and he went with them to the queen, and said to her, "You are aware what terrible things we have survived, and the many wars and battles which we fought in support of Alexander and his father Hyrcanus. Therefore it was not right to trample on our rights, to lift up the hand of our enemies over us, and to lower our dignity. An incident like this will be reported to Aretas and your other enemies, who have experienced our bravery and have not been able to resist us, and their hearts have been filled with the fear of us. When they find out what you have done to us, they will imagine we are conspiring against you, and if confirmed, they will trust that we will betray you. Also, we will not agree to be slaughtered by the Pharisees, like sheep. Therefore, either restrain their hatred from us or allow us to leave the city into some of the towns of Judea."

CHAPTER 32

She answered them, "Do this, so their annoyance with you may be prevented."

So the Sadducees left the city, and their leaders departed with the warriors who followed them. They took their cattle to the towns of Judea which they had selected, lived in them, and joined with the Hasideans.

Chapter 33

After this, Alexandra caught a disease from which she died. When it became clear she would not recover, her son Aristobulus left Jerusalem at night, accompanied by his servant. He met with one of his friends at Gabbatha,[1] a leader of the Sadducees, and traveled with him to the cities where the Sadducees lived. He told them his purpose and exhorted them to go out with him and be his allies in a war against his brother and the Pharisees, and to appoint him king. They agreed to this, openly betraying Alexandra, and collecting men from every quarter to join Aristobulus.

When reports of this reached Hyrcanus, the son of Alexandra, the high priest and the leaders of the Pharisees went to Alexandra, sick as she was, and told her the situation, informing her of the great fear which they had for her and her son Hyrcanus, from Aristobulus and those who were with him.

She replied, "I am truly near death, so it is more proper and wise for me to attend to my own concerns. What can I do, in this situation? My men, and my goods, and my arms, are with you and in your hands. Therefore give the commands that seem right to you, imploring the aid of God in your matters, and asking deliverance from Him."

CHAPTER 33

Then she died. She was seventy-three years old and had reigned for nine years.

Chapter 33 Notes

1 Arabic: ğbāṭā (جباتا)

Gbtå (ܓܒܬܐ) is an Aramaic word that translates as 'cheese,' and was the name of a place inside Jerusalem, although the modern location is debated. The name was transliterated into Greek as Gabbatha (Γαββαθα) in the Gospel of John, who also provided the Greek name of Lithostrôton (Λιθόστρωτον), meaning 'covered in cobblestones.'

Chapter 34

When Aristobulus left Jerusalem in the days of Alexandra, he left his wife and children in Jerusalem. However, when the news of his departure reached Alexandra, she placed them under house arrest, stationing a guard with them. When Alexandra was dead, Hyrcanus brought them to him, was kind to them, and took care of them, so they would save him from his brother if his brother was victorious.

Aristobulus commanded a great army near the Jordan, and Hyrcanus went out against him with an army of Pharisees. When the two armies engaged, great numbers of Hyrcanus' army were killed, and Hyrcanus took the remainder of his army and fled. Aristobulus and his soldiers pursued, killing everyone they caught, except those who surrendered themselves. Hyrcanus retreated into the sacred city, and Aristobulus and his army followed. He surrounded it on every side with his camp and contemplated ways to destroy the fortifications. The Sanhedrin of Judea, and the elders of the priests, went out to him, and forbade him from doing what he had planned, asking him to forget whatever hostile feeling he had towards his brother, to which he agreed.

It was agreed between them that Aristobulus should be king over Judea, and Hyrcanus should be the high priest in the temple of God, and equal to the king in

Chapter 34

dignity. Aristobulus agreed to these terms, and entered the city, and spoke with his brother in the temple of God. They made an oath to ratify the terms the Sanhedrin had decided on. So Aristobulus was made king, and Hyrcanus was considered equal to him. Men were at peace, and the affairs of these two brothers were properly ordered, and their people and country became tranquil.

Chapter 35

There was a man among the Judeans, of the sons of those who traveled out of Babylon with Ezra the priest, named Antipater.[1] He was wise, prudent, acute, brave, and high-minded, of a good disposition, kind, and courteous; also rich, and possessing many houses, goods, and flocks.

King Alexander had made this man governor of the country of the Edomites, from whom he had taken a wife. With her, he had four sons, named Faisal,[2] Herod (who reigned over Judea), Pheroras, and Josephus. Afterward, having left the mountains of Seir, (that is, the country of the Edomites), in the days of Alexander, he dwelt in the city of the sacred temple, and Hyrcanus loved him, and was much inclined towards him. Because of this, Aristobulus wanted to kill him, but, did not succeed at this.

Antipater was terrified of Aristobulus, and for that reason began secretly to plot against Aristobulus' kingdom. He went to the chief men of the kingdom and after getting from them a pledge of secrecy respecting the matters he wanted to discuss, he began to talk to them of the infamous life of Aristobulus, his tyranny, his impiety, and the bloodshed which he had caused, and his usurpation of the throne, of which his elder brother was more worthy.

CHAPTER 35

Then he warned them to be aware of the response of the great and good God if they did not take away the tyrant's rule, and restored what was due to their rightful sovereign. There were none of the chief men whom he did not convince to submit to Hyrcanus, winning them over from their obedience to Aristobulus. Hyrcanus knew nothing about this, but Antipater claimed it was his plan, and he was unwilling to discuss it before it was established.

Therefore, when the chief men had agreed to the plan, he went to Hyrcanus, and said to him, "Your brother is afraid of you because he sees that his rule will not be secure as long as you are alive. Because of this, he is looking for an opportunity to kill you, and will not allow you to live."

But Hyrcanus did not believe him, because of the purity and sincerity of his heart. Antipater told him this again and again. He gave large sums of money to the people that Hyrcanus trusted the most so that they should tell him similar things, but to be careful that he should not get the idea that they had been speaking with Antipater about it. Hyrcanus believed their words and was convinced to devise a scheme to save himself from his brother.

Therefore, when Antipater spoke with him again regarding this, he informed him that the truth of his words was now known to him and that he knew that he had advised him well. He asked his opinion regarding this business, and Antipater advised him to leave the city and go to someone he trusted who could aid and assist him. Antipater went to Aretas III[3] and made an agreement with him to receive Hyrcanus as a guest when he came since he was afraid of living with his brother. Aretas III was excited and was informed about the rest of the conspiracy.

He made an agreement with Antipater that under no circumstances would he deliver Hyrcanus and Antipater to their enemies, and that he would assist and protect them. He returned to Jerusalem and told Hyrcanus what he had done, and how he had made an agreement with Aretas III regarding their going to him. Then both of them left the city at night, went to Aretas III, and remained with him for some time. Then Antipater began trying to persuade Aretas III to take his army with Hyrcanus, to defeat and capture his brother Aristobulus. Aretas III decided against this plan, as he was afraid that his army was not strong enough to defeat Aristobulus.

Antipater continued to show him how trade was bad because of Aristobulus and to urge him on by pointing out the wealth to be gained, the great fame that he would acquire, and the memory that he would leave behind. Eventually, he consented to march, but on the condition that Hyrcanus would return to him the cities and towns that had belonged to his father, which Alexander had taken away.

Once Hyrcanus agreed and completed a treaty, Aretas III marched into Judea, and went to Hyrcanus with him, with fifty thousand cavalry and infantry. Aristobulus went out and engaged them, and when the fighting became fierce, many of Aristobulus' army switched sides to Hyrcanus. When Aristobulus saw it, he sounded a retreat and returned to his camp, afraid his whole army could defect to the enemy, and he would be taken prisoner. In the evening, Aristobulus left the camp on his own and returned to the sacred city.

In the morning, when his army found out he had abandoned them, most joined with Hyrcanus, and the rest dispersed to their homes. Hyrcanus, Aretas III, and Antipater continued straight to the city of the sacred temple, leading a large army, and they found that Aristobulus had prepared for a siege. He had closed the gates of the city and had placed men on the ramparts to defend them. Hyrcanus and Aretas III camped with their forces around the city and besieged it.

Chapter 35 Notes

1 There are no Judahite records of Antipater's lineage, and the author appears to be trying to synchronize the conflicting reports of their lineage found in the writing of both Nicolaus of Damascus and Josephus. Nicolaus was the court historian in the time of King Herod, who reported that the family was descended from the Judaites that accompanied Ezra back from Babylon. Josephus, writing after the Herodian dynasty had lost power, claimed that Antipater was the descendent of Edomites who had been forcibly converted to Judaism by John Hyrcanus, and was, therefore, a 'half-Jew.'

2 Arabic: fṣāåylws (فصائيلوس)

Herod commemorated his brother Pṣål (פצאל) by building a watch tower in the Jordan Valley, north of Jericho, and naming it after him. A Palestinian village at the site continues to be called fṣāyl (فصايل), normally translated into English as Fasayil. The original name is Arabic, and translates as 'arbiter.' It was translated into Greek as Phasaêlos (Φασάηλος), which appears to be the origin of the Arabic name used in the text. The Arabic spelling in the text is likely derived from a Palestinian Arabic source text, as the name has no intrinsic meaning in Hebrew or Aramaic, and therefore would have probably been transliterated into Aramaic from Greek as Pṣålws (פצאלוס). This translation uses the most common transliteration of the Arabic name: Faisal.

3 Arabic: ḥārṭàm (حارثةع)

Based on other records of the events, this is a reference to Hrtt III (תתרת), who also officially spelled his name as Aretas (Αρέτας) in Greek. He was the king of Nabataea between 87 and 62 BC. The Arabic spelling in the text is not the proper Arabic spelling of the name, which is ḥārṭà (حارثة), and appears to be the Arabic transliteration of ḥrtm (חרתם), a Palestinian Aramaic transliteration of Aretan (ⲁⲣⲉⲧⲁⲛ), the Coptic spelling of Aretas. This suggests the Palestinian author partially drew from Egyptian sources.

Chapter 36

Now it happened at that time, that General Pompey[1] of the Roman army, went out to fight with Tigranes[2] the Armenian, for the citizens of Damascus, Hamath, Aleppo, and the rest of those in Syria who were subject to the Armenians, had recently rebelled against the Romans. Because of that Pompey had sent Scaurus to Damascus and to its territories to take possession of them, which was reported to Aristobulus and Hyrcanus. Therefore Aristobulus sent ambassadors to Scaurus, and a lot of money, requesting him to come to him with an army and assist him against Hyrcanus. Hyrcanus also sent ambassadors to him, requesting his aid against Aristobulus, but he did not send him a tribute.

Scaurus refused to go to either of them, but he wrote to Aretas III, ordering him to remove his army from the city of the sacred temple, and forbidding him to help Hyrcanus against his brother. He threatened that he would come into his country with an army of Romans and Syrians unless he obeyed. When this letter reached Aretas III, he immediately left the city, and Hyrcanus also left. Aristobulus pursued them with a number of his soldiers, caught up to them, and attacked them, and a great number of the Arabs were killed in the battle, and very many Judeans. Then Aristobulus returned to the sacred city.

CHAPTER 36

In the meantime, Pompey had arrived in Damascus, and Aristobulus sent to him, by the hand of a man named Nicomedes, a garden or a vineyard made of gold[3] with a value of five hundred talents as a rich tribute, and asked his assistance against Hyrcanus. Hyrcanus sent Antipater to Pompey, with a similar request, and Pompey was inclined to help Aristobulus. When Antipater saw this, he looked for an opportunity that he might speak with Pompey alone, and said to him, "In truth, the tribute you have received from Aristobulus is not be returned to him, however, you should not assist him. Hyrcanus offers you twice as much, and Aristobulus will not be able to make the Judeans subjects to you, but Hyrcanus will do this."

Pompey believed the situation was as Antipater had said, and he celebrated, thinking he could bring the Judeans under his dominion. Therefore he replied to Antipater, "I will assist your friend against Aristobulus, however, I will pretend to help him against you, so he will trust me. As I am sure, that as soon as he finds out that I am aiding his brother against him, he will lie to all his men, and will take care of himself, and this business will take much longer.

I will send for him and will return with him into the sacred city, and then will take actions so your friend will obtain his right, but with this condition, that he will pay us an annual tribute."

After this, he sent for Nicomedes, and said to him, "Go to your master, and tell him, that I have consented to his request. Take him my letter, and say to him, that he must hurry to me without delay, as I will wait for him."

He wrote the following letter to Aristobulus:

From General Pompey of the Roman army to King Aristobulus, heir to the throne and high priesthood, health be to you.

Your garden or vineyard of gold has arrived, and I have received it, and have sent it to the elder and the senators, which they have accepted and have placed in the temple at Rome, returning you thanks.

They have written, moreover, that I should assist you, and recognize you as king over the Judeans. Therefore, if you think it is acceptable, come to me as soon as possible, so I may go up with you to the sacred city, and fulfill your wishes, and I will do so.

Nicomedes traveled to Aristobulus Pompey's letter, and Antipater returned to Hyrcanus to tell him of Pompey's promise and advise him to go to Damascus. So Hyrcanus went to Damascus, and so did Aristobulus, and they met in Damascus in the audience room of Pompey. Antipater and the Sanhedrin of the Judeans said to

Pompey, "Know, most illustrious general, that this Aristobulus has been lying to us, and has usurped by the sword the kingdom of his brother Hyrcanus, who is more worthy of it as he is the older brother, and also of a better character and way of life. It was not enough for him to oppress his brother, but he has oppressed all the nations which are around us, unjustly shedding their blood and pillaging their property, and maintaining enmities between us and them, something we abhor."

Then a thousand elders arose in agreement with his words.

Aristobulus replied, "Honestly, my brother is a better man than I am, but I did not seek the throne, until I saw that all those who had been subject to our father Alexander were being treacherous with us after his death, knowing the inability of my brother.

When I looked into it, I believed that it was my duty to assume the throne, in that I was better in matters of war, and therefore was better suited for preserving the kingdom. I went to war with all those who dealt treacherously with us, and reduced them to subservience, as was the command of our father before his death."

He also brought out witnesses who attested to the truth of his words.

After this, Pompey departed from the city of Damascus and journeyed to the sacred temple. Antipater quietly sent messages to the inhabitants of the cities that Aristobulus had conquered, urging them to complain to Pompey, explaining the tyranny that he had imposed on them, which they did. Pompey ordered him to write them a testimonial of their freedom and to agree that he would not trouble them again. This he did, and the nations were released from their subservience to Judea.

When Aristobulus understood what Pompey had done to him, he and his men departed from Pompey's army came at night without letting him know, and returned to the city of the sacred temple. Pompey followed them to the city of the sacred temple, where he encamped. When he saw the height of the walls, and the strength of its buildings, and the numbers of men who were in it, and the mountains which surrounded it, he understood that flattery and cunning would not be enough against Aristobulus.

Therefore, he sent ambassadors to him, requesting that he come out to meet with him, and promising him safe passage. Aristobulus went out to him, and Pompey received politely, not saying a word about what had happened. Aristobulus told Pompey, "I want you to aid me against my brother, giving my enemies no power over me. For this, you may have whatever you wish."

Pompey replied, "If this is what you want, bring to me whatever money and precious stones are in the temple, and I will put you in possession of what you wish."

Aristobulus said to him, "I will do this."

Pompey sent a captain named Gabinius with many men, to receive whatever of gold and jewels there was in the temple. But the citizens and the priests refused to permit this, and they resisted Gabinius, killing many of his men and his friends, and driving him out of the city. This made Pompey angry with Aristobulus, and he arrested him.

Then he marched with his army, to force his way into the city, but a great number of the citizens came out and prevented him from doing this, by killing great numbers of his men. In truth, the numbers, the spirit, and the bravery of the people that he witnessed frightened him. Being alarmed by this, he decided to leave them, having not resolved the dispute in the city between the supporters of Aristobulus and the supporters of Hyrcanus. Some of them wanted to open the gates to Pompey, but others were opposed to this, and began they fighting over it. This situation increased rather than diminished, and the fighting intensified. Pompey noticed and sent some of his army to the gate of the city, and

CHAPTER 36

some of the people opened a wicket gate to him. He entered and took possession of the king's palace, but could not enter the temple because the priests had locked the doors, and had secured the approaches with armed men.

Against these, he sent men to attack them from every direction, and they caused them to flee. His supporters entered the temple, by climbing the wall and dropping down into it, and then opened its gates after killing many of the priests. Then Pompey came and entered into it, and greatly admired the beauty and splendor which he saw, and was astonished when he saw its riches and the precious stones which were in it. He decided not to take anything out of it, and he commanded the priests to remove the dead from the temple and to offer sacrifices according to the ceremonies of their country.

Chapter 36 Notes

1 Arabic: nyyās (نيياس). Translation: Gnaeus

Gnaeus Pompeius Magnus, generally known as Pompey in modern literature, led the Roman army in the Third Mithridatic War, between 73 and 63 BC. The text generally refers to him as Gnaeus, however, does switch to Pompey (بومبيوس) a few times, suggesting the author was combining different sources. In this translation, the name is standardized to 'Pompey.'

2 Arabic: dykrānws (ديكرانوس). Translation: Tigranes

Tigranes II (Τιγράνης / Sḥqn̄u̇) was the king of Armenia between 95 and 55 BC.

3 Josephus recorded that some described it as a golden vine while others described it as a golden garden. He claimed to have seen it at the Temple of Zeus Capitolinus in Rome, and it was inscribed with the words "The gift of Alexander, the king of Judea."

Chapter 37

Having resolved the situation, Pompey appointed Hyrcanus to be king and took away his brother Aristobulus in chains. He ordered that the Judeans should have no dominion over those nations who had been subdued by their kings before his arrival, and he exacted a tribute from the city of the sacred temple, and an agreement with Hyrcanus, that he should receive inauguration from the Romans every year. He departed, taking Aristobulus with him, and two of his sons and his daughters. He had another son named Alexander, whom Pompey could not arrest as he had fled. Pompey left in his previous position in the city of the sacred temple, Hyrcanus and Antipater, along with his own colleague Scaurus.

Chapter 38

After Pompey had left for Rome, Hyrcanus and Antipater marched against the Arabs, to bring them under the dominion of Rome. The Arabs submitted, trusting Antipater intimately, and regarding his advice greatly. Through this, Antipater planned to reconcile the Romans to him.

When Alexander the son of Aristobulus saw the expedition of Hyrcanus, Antipater, and Scaurus, against the Arabs leave to travel a great distance from the sacred city, he traveled there. He entered the palace and took the money set aside for repairing the city wall which Pompey had broken down, and he raised an army and reorganized everything he wanted before Hyrcanus and his army could return to the city of the sacred temple. When they returned, he went out to meet them, engaged them, and caused them to flee.

Chapter 39

Gabinius traveled from Rome to live in the land of Syria, to govern it, and he heard what Alexander the son of Aristobulus had done, by building up that which Pompey had pulled down, and by opposing his successor and killing his friends.

Therefore, he immediately traveled to Jerusalem, and Hyrcanus and his supporters joined him. Alexander went out to meet them with ten thousand infantrymen and fifteen hundred cavalrymen and engaged them, but they routed him and killed some of his friends.

He fled to a city named Alexandrium in the land of Judea, which he fortified with his army. Hyrcanus and Gabinius, and their armies, marched against him and besieged him. Alexander went out against them, attacked them, and slaughtered many of their men.

Marcus Antonius marched against him and forced him to retreat back into Alexandrium. Alexander's mother went out to Gabinius to calm his anger and implored him to grant her son Alexander his life. Gabinius agreed to this point, and Alexander went out to him, but Gabinius put him to death. He thought it proper to divide the territories of Judea into five parts. One is the land of Jerusalem and the region around it. Over this part, Hyrcanus was made governor. Another part is Gadira and the region around it. The third is Jericho and the plains. The fourth is Amathus[1] in the land of Judea. The fifth is Sephoris.[2] By this, he intended to remove wars and sedition from the land of Judea, but they did not end.

Chapter 39 Notes

1 Arabic: ȯmāṯws (أماثوس). Translation: Amathus

Amathus, spelled variously as Amathous (Ἀμαθοῦς) by Josephus, Ammathous (Ἀμμαθοὺς) by Eusebius, ȯmtw (עמתו) in the Jerusalem Talmud, was a city east of the Jordan River, in modern-day Jordan. It is believed to have been at the ruins known as Tell Ammata.

2 Arabic: ṣfwryà (صفورية). Translation: Sepphoris

Sepphoris (Σέπφωρις) was the Greek transliteration of the Hebrew and Aramaic name Tzippori (צִפּוֹרִי). Tzippori was an ancient town in central Galilee, where, according to Christian tradition, Jesus' mother's family was from. According to the Talmud, it is the town that was called Kitron (קִטְרוֹן) in the Masoretic book of Judges, an ancient town of Canaanites that continued to live among the Israelites after the time of Joshua.

Chapter 40

Aristobulus schemed cunningly until he had escaped from Rome with his son Antigonus, and he traveled back to the land of Judea. When Aristobulus showed himself in public, a great multitude of men flocked around him.

He selected eight thousand and marched against Gabinius, and engaged him. Many of the Roman soldiers were killed, however, seven thousand of his own men also fell. One thousand escaped, and the enemy army pursued him. He and those with him did not stop fighting until all of his men were killed. There was no one left, just him alone, and he fought furiously until he collapsed from his wounds. He was captured and led to Gabinius, who ordered him to be taken care of while he healed. Then he sent him in chains to Rome.

He remained locked up in prison until the reign of Caesar, who released him from prison and bestowed on him gifts and favors. He gave him two generals and twelve thousand men, and sent him into the land of Judea, to remove the Judeans from Pompey's alliance, and make them loyal to Caesar, as by then Pompey was governor of the land of Egypt.

The report of Aristobulus and his faction reached Hyrcanus, who was terrified and wrote to Antipater to avert his power from him by his customary schemes.

CHAPTER 40

Antipater sent some of the chief men of Jerusalem, giving one of them poison, ordering him to quietly poison Aristobulus. They met him in the land of Syria pretending they were ambassadors to him from the sacred city, and he received them joyfully, and they ate and drank with him. Those men schemed until they had poisoned him. He died and was buried in the land of Syria.

The era of his reign, until he was taken prisoner the first time, was three and a half years. He was a man of courage, weight, and excellent disposition.

Gabinius had written to the senate, to release his two sons to their mother, since she had requested it, and which they did. However, it happened that when Pompey had traveled a great distance from Jerusalem, they broke their treaty of obedience to the Romans. Therefore Gabinius went against them, engaged them, conquered them, and reduced them again to submission to the Romans.

In the meanwhile, the land of Egypt had rebelled against Ptolemy, and expelled him from his royal city, refusing to pay tribute to the Romans. Ptolemy had written to Gabinius that he should come and help him against the Egyptians, so he could bring them again into subjection to the Romans. So Gabinius marched out of the land of Syria and wrote to Hyrcanus to meet him with an army, so they might go to Ptolemy. Antipater traveled with a large army to Gabinius, and met him in Damascus, congratulating him on the victory which he had achieved over the Persians. Gabinius ordered him to rush to assist Ptolemy, which he did, and fought against the Egyptians, and slaughtered a very large amount of them. Afterward, Gabinius joined them, placed Ptolemy back on his throne, and then traveled back to the sacred city and renewed Hyrcanus' sovereignty. Then he returned to Rome.

Chapter 41

When Gabinius had returned to Rome, the Persians betrayed the Romans, and Crassus marched with a large army into Syria, and came to Jerusalem, requiring the priests should give him whatever money there was in the temple of God.

They inquired, "How is this lawful for you when Pompey, Gabinius, and others have believed it unlawful?"

Yet he answered, "I must do it in any event."

Eleazar the priest said to him, "Swear to me that you will not lay your hands on anything which belongs to it, and I will give you three hundred minas[1] of gold."

He swore to him that he would take nothing from the treasure of the temple of God if he would provide this tribute. Eleazar gave him a bar of worked gold. It had been inserted into the wall of the treasury of the temple, and the old veils of the temple were laid on it each year when the new veils replaced them. The gold bar weighed three hundred minas, but it was covered with the veils as they accumulated over the years and was unknown to everyone other than Eleazar. After receiving the bar, Crassus broke his word, going back from the agreement he made with Eleazar, and he seized all the treasures of the temple. He pillaged all the wealth that was within it, adding up to two thousand talents. This money had been accumulating from the rebuilding of the temple until that time, from the spoils of the kings of Judea and their offerings, and also from the presents that the kings of the Gentiles had sent. They had multiplied and increased over the years, but he took it all. Then the awful Crassus went off with the wealth and his army into the country of the Persians. They defeated him and his army in battle, killing them all in a single day, and the Persian army took as spoils everything that was in Crassus' camp.

After this, they marched into the land of Syria, which they occupied, detaching it from submission to the Romans. When the Romans heard of it, they sent a renowned general named Cassius with a great army. He entered the land of Syria and drove out the Persians who were in it. Then he proceeded to the sacred city, and he saved Hyrcanus from the war that the Judeans were waging against him, reconciling the parties.

Afterward, he passed over the Euphrates, fought with the Persians, and brought them back to their subjection to the Romans. He also reduced to submission the twenty-two kings that Pompey had subdued and reduced under obedience to the Romans everything in the lands of the east.

Chapter 41 Notes

1 Arabic: myn (مين). Translation: minas

The mana (𒈠𒈾) was originally a Sumerian unit of weight equal to approximately 500 grams. It was adopted as the Akkadian manû (𒈠𒈾𒌁), a standardized measurement equal to 60 shekels. The manû was used in Mesopotamian cultures for thousands of years, although the Neo-Assyrians doubled the weight of the manû. It had been adopted into Canaanite by the Late Bronze Age, where it was spelled as mn (𐎎𐎐) in Ugaritic. In the Iron Age, it was adopted into Aramaic as mnh (מנה), which was itself adopted into Hebrew as manah (מָנֶה). The Greeks also adopted the Semitic name as mna (μνᾶ), however, the value was not consistent in different Greek city-states.

Greeks and Romans generally traded in silver minas, although gold minas are also documented. At the time, gold was valued around 10 times silver. In the era the events took place, the value of the mina would have ranged between 430 grams and 630 grams of silver, or 100 sheep, or around 40 kilograms of grain. In Rome, a common house was generally around 40 minas, while a slave was generally around 20 minas. Therefore, the priest was offering a value of approximately 75 houses in Rome.

Chapter 42

It is reported that there was in Rome a woman who was pregnant, and being near to her delivery, and racked with the most violent pains of childbirth, died, but as the child was in motion, the belly of the mother was cut open and it was lifted out. It lived, and grew, and was named Julius, because he was born in the fifth month, and was called Caesar, because the belly of his mother, from where he was extracted, was ripped open. When the elder of Rome sent Pompey into the east, he also sent Caesar into the west, to subdue certain nations which had revolted from the Romans. Caesar went and conquered them, reduced them to subjugation to the Romans, and returned to Rome with great glory. His fame increased, and his affairs became much renowned, and he became excessively prideful, to the point that he requested the Romans to name him king.

The elder and governors answered him, "Truly our fathers took an oath in the days of Tarquin the king, who had raped another man's wife, abusing her so the man would not enjoy her, that they would not give the title of king to any of those who should be placed at the head of their affairs, on account of which oath, we are not able to grant you in this thing."

Therefore he stirred up sedition, and waged furious battles against Rome, slaughtering many people until he seized the throne of the Romans, and proclaimed himself king, putting a crown on his head. From then onward, they were called kings of the Romans, from their kingdom. They were also called Caesars.

When Pompey heard what Caesar had done, that he had killed the three hundred and twenty governors, he amassed his armies and marched into Cappadocia. Caesar went to meet him and engaged him, defeated him, killed him, and gained possession of all territories of the Romans. After this, Caesar went into the province of Syria, where Mithridates the Armenians met him with his army. He assured him that he had come as an ally, and was ready to attack whatever enemies he should command. Caesar ordered him to march into Egypt, and Mithridates marched until he arrived in Ascalon.

Hyrcanus was terrified of Caesar, because his submission to Pompey was well known, and Caesar had killed him. Therefore, he quickly sent Antipater with a brave army to assist Mithridates, and Antipater marched quickly to him and aided him against one of the cities of Egypt, and they captured it. However, when they were departing from there, they found an army of Egyptian Judahites, blocking Mithridates from entering farther into Egypt. Antipater gave them a letter from Hyrcanus, ordering them to stop opposing Mithridates, the friend of Caesar, and they stepped aside. The rest marched until they came to the city of the then-reigning king, who came out to them with all the armies of Egypt, and when they engaged with him, he defeated and routed them. Mithridates turned his back and fled, but became surrounded by the Egyptian forces. Antipater saved him from death, as Antipater and his men did not stop battling the Egyptians, but instead routed them and conquered the whole country of Egypt.

Mithridates wrote to Caesar, explaining what Antipater had done, what battles he had endured, and what wounds he had received. He claimed that the conquest of the country was to be considered Antipater's victory, not his own and that he had reduced the Egyptians to submission to Caesar. When Caesar had read the letter of Mithridates, he commended Antipater for his exploits and decided to advance and exalt him. After this, Mithridates and Antipater went to Caesar, who then was in Damascus; and he obtained from Caesar whatever he liked, and he promised him whatever he wanted.

Chapter 43

Antigonus the son of Aristobulus went to Caesar and told him the expedition of Aristobulus his father to attack Pompey, and how obedient and helpful he was to him. Then he told him, "Hyrcanus and Antipater secretly sent a man to my father to assassinate him by poison, intending to help Pompey against your allies."

Caesar sent for Antipater and questioned him about this, and Antipater replied, "Certainly I did obey Pompey, because then he was the ruler, and he conferred benefits on me. However, I did not fight the Egyptians for the sake of Pompey, who is already dead. I did not struggle to defeat them and reduce them to submission to Pompey. I did this out of duty to Caesar, and that I might reduce them to submit to him."

Then Antipater uncovered his head and his hands, and said, "These wounds, which are on my head and body, testify that my affection and obedience to Caesar are greater than my affection and obedience to Pompey, as I did not risk myself in the days of Pompey, to the things to that I have risked in the days of king Caesar."

Caesar replied to him, "Peace be to you, and to all your friends, bravest of the Judeans, for you have truly shown fortitude, magnanimity, obedience, and affection towards us."

CHAPTER 43

From that time Caesar increased in affection towards Antipater, elevated him above all his friends, promoted him to be general of his armies, and took him with him into the land of the Persians. He saw his bravery and his successful expeditions, and he had more and more respect for him. Eventually, he brought him back into the land of Judea, covered with honors and awarded with a post of authority.

Caesar marched to Rome, having settled the affairs of Hyrcanus, who rebuilt the walls of the sacred city, and conducted himself well in the view of the people. He was a good man, endowed with virtues, of irreproachable life, but his inability in wars was notorious to all men.

Chapter 44

Hyrcanus sent ambassadors to Caesar, with a letter about renewing of the treaty between him and the Romans. When Hyrcanus' ambassadors visited Caesar, he ordered them to be seated in his presence, an honor which he had not conferred on any of the other ambassadors of kings who visited him.

He treated them well, expediting their business, and dictated the following letter in reply to Hyrcanus' letter:

From Caesar, king of kings, to the princes of the Romans who are at Tyre and Sidon, peace be with you.

I want you to know, that a letter of Hyrcanus the son of Alexander, both kings of Judea, has been brought to me. I rejoiced at its arrival, because of the continued goodwill which both he and his people declare that they have towards me and the Roman nation. The truth of his words I have proved by the fact that he previously sent Antipater a Judean captain, and their cavalry, with Mithridates my friend, who were attacked by the Egyptian army. He saved Mithridates from death, conquered for us all the land of Egypt, and reduced the Egyptians to submission to the Romans. He also marched with me into the land of Persia, serving as a volunteer.

Therefore, I order that all the inhabitants of the sea coast, from Gaza as far as Sidon, shall pay all the tributes which they owe us, every year, to the temple of the great God which is in Jerusalem, not including the citizens of

Sidon. Let them pay to it, as per their tribute, twenty thousand five hundred and fifty libras of wheat every year. I also order, that Laodicea and its possessions, and all things which were in the hand of the kings of Judea, all the way to the bank of the Euphrates, with all those places which the Hasmonaeans conquered beyond Jordan, be restored to Hyrcanus the son of Alexander king of Judea.

All these things, his fathers had conquered with their swords, and Pompey unjustly took them away in the time of Aristobulus. From this time and throughout the future, let them belong to Hyrcanus, and to the succeeding kings of Judea. This treaty is for me, and for every one of the kings of Rome who succeed me. Whoever will break it, or any part of it, may God destroy him by the sword, and may his house and his government be made desolate and be cut down!

When you read this, my letter, engrave it in letters on brass tables in the language of the Romans and in their alphabet, and in the language of the Greeks and in their alphabet, and place the tables in a prominent place in the temples at Tyre and Sidon, so every person may be able to see them and may understand what I have appointed for Hyrcanus and the Judeans.

Chapter 45

There were with Caesar two of Pompey's friends, one called Cassius, and the other Brutus, and they plotted to kill Caesar. So they concealed themselves in the temple in Rome which he had set aside for himself to pray in. When he entered, he was relaxed, believing he was safe, and not paying attention, when they attacked him and killed him. Cassius seized the throne, gathered a large army, and transported it over the sea, afraid of Caesar's allies should he remain in Rome.

He marched into the land of Asia and laid waste to it, and from there he entered into the land of Judea. Antipater wanted to attack him, but when he saw that his army was not big enough, he made peace with him. Cassius demanded a tribute of seven hundred talents of gold from the land of Judea, and Antipater allowed himself to be held in custody until the money was raised. He ordered his son Herod to raise it in the country of Judea and to bring it to Cassius. After receiving it, he marched into the country of Macedonia and remained there, because of his fear of the Romans.

Chapter 46

The princes of Judea had decided to kill Antipater and secretly contracted a man called Malchiah. Malchiah agreed to the plan, but the plan was delayed for a long time. Antipater heard of it and arrested Malchiah intent on executing him, but Malchiah cleared himself in the sight of Antipater of what he had been accused of and swore to him that the accusation was groundless. Antipater believed him and dismissed all suspicion from him.

Nevertheless, Malchiah had given a large amount of money to Hyrcanus' cup-bearer, who agreed to poison Antipater while he was in the king's presence at a banquet. The cup-bearer did this, and King Antipater died that very day, and this was not by the design, nor with the knowledge of the king. When Antipater was dead, Hyrcanus substituted Malchiah in his place.

Chapter 47

When Herod the son of Antipater was informed that Malchiah had caused his father's death, he wanted to openly attack Malchiah, but his brother stopped him from doing this, advising that he should be removed through strategy. Herod went to Cassius and told him what Malchiah had done, and he replied, "When I go to Tyre, and Hyrcanus comes to meet with me he'll bring Malchiah with him. Attack him and kill him then."

Therefore, when Cassius went to Tyre, Hyrcanus went to join him, taking along Malchiah with him, to stand together in his presence. Cassius had invited them to a feast, along with his other friends. Herod also was standing with his brother among the companions of Hyrcanus, and Herod had made an agreement with some of the servants to kill Malchiah when a signal was given by a wink of the eye. (Cassius had ordered his servants to do whatever Herod told them.)

When Hyrcanus had eaten and drank with his friends, they went to nap in the afternoon, and after they woke up, Hyrcanus ordered someone to set up a couch for him in the open air, in front of the entrance of the banquet hall where they had slept. Then he sat himself down and commanded Malchiah to sit with him. He also ordered Herod and his brother to be seated, and Cassius' servants stood near Hyrcanus. When Herod

CHAPTER 47

winked against Malchiah, they immediately attacked him and killed him, and Hyrcanus was terrified and fainted in fear.

After Cassius' attendants had left, and the dead Malchiah had been carried out, Hyrcanus woke up and asked Herod why Malchiah had been killed. Herod answered, "I am completely ignorant, and do not know the cause."

Hyrcanus held his peace, and never again asked regarding the matter.

Cassius marched into Macedonia, to meet Octavian the son of Caesar's brother, and Antony the general of his army, as they had set out from Rome with a great army in search of Cassius.

Chapter 48

When Octavian had marched into Macedonia, Cassius went out to meet him, and engaged him, and Cassius was forced to retreat. Octavian pursued him, and entirely defeated and killed him. Octavian won the kingdom in place of his uncle Caesar, and he also was named Caesar, after the name of his uncle.

When Hyrcanus heard of the death of Cassius, he sent ambassadors with gifts, money, and jewels, to Augustus and Antony, and he wrote to him, asking for a renewal of the treaty which had been negotiated with Caesar.

He asked that all the enslaved Judeans who were in his kingdom, and those who had been made slaves in the days of Cassius, be released and that all Judeans be permitted to return to the land of Judea from the lands of the Greeks, and the land of Asia, without requiring any ransom, or redemption, or any obstacle being placed in the way by anyone.

When the ambassadors of Hyrcanus went to Augustus with their gifts and the letter, he honored the ambassadors, accepted the gifts, and agreed to all things that Hyrcanus had asked. He wrote the following letter:

From Augustus, king of kings, and Antony his colleague, to Hyrcanus king of Judea,

Health be to you. Your letter has reached us, at which we rejoiced. We have sent that which you wished, regarding the renewal of the treaty, the writing to all our provinces, which extend from the land of India to the western ocean.

That which delayed us from writing sooner to you regarding the renewal of the treaty was our operation to subdue Cassius, that despicable tyrant, who, acted evilly towards Caesar, that luminary of the world, and murdered him. We have fought him with all our strength, until the great and good God rendered us victorious, and caused him to fall into our hands, whom we have put to death. We have also killed his colleague Brutus, and we have rescued the country of Asia from his hands, after he had laid waste to it, and had exterminated its inhabitants.

He did not adhere to any treaty, honor any temple, nor do justice to the oppressed, nor pity any Judean or any of our other subjects. He and his followers acted wickedly and did many evils to all men through oppression and tyranny. Therefore, God has turned their malice back on their own heads, delivering them up, with those who were allied to them.

Rejoice now, King Hyrcanus, and other Judeans, inhabitants of the holy land, and priests who are in the temple in Jerusalem. Let them accept the gift which we have sent to the most glorious temple, and pray for Augustus forever. We have written also to all our provinces, that there should remain in none of them any of the Judeans, whether male slave or female slave, but that all should be freed without price or ransom, and that no one should hinder them from returning into the land of Judea. This by command of Augustus, and likewise of Antony his colleague.

Additionally, he wrote to his allies at Tyre, Sidon, and other places, to restore whatever they had taken out of the land of Judea in the days of that terrible Cassius, and to treat the Judeans peaceably, and not to oppose them in anything, and to do for them whatever Caesar had decreed in his treaty with them.

Antony remained in the land of Syria, and Cleopatra, the queen of Egypt, came to him, and they were married. She was a wise woman, skilled in magical arts and other arts, by which she seduced him, and got possession of his heart to that degree that he could deny her nothing.

At this same time, a hundred of the chief men of Judea went to Antony and complained about Herod and his brother Faisal, the sons of Antipater, saying, "They have now taken everything belonging to Hyrcanus, and there remains to him nothing of the kingdom except the name. This is hidden because our lord is held captive."

However, when Antony inquired of Hyrcanus regarding that which they had reported to him, Hyrcanus stated that they were lying, and cleared Herod and his brother from their charge. Antony rejoiced at this, as he respected them greatly, and he loved them.

Moreover, when others at a later time complained to him of Herod and his brother, while he was visiting Tyre, he not only refused to consider their words, but put some of them to death, and threw the rest into prison. He elevated the dignity of Herod and his brother, doing them services, and sent them back to Jerusalem with great honor.

Antony himself went into the land of the Parthians, defeated and subdued them, and then returned to Rome.

Chapter 49

When Augustus and Antony had arrived at Rome, Antigonus went to the king of Parthia and promised him a thousand talents of gold coins, and eight hundred virgins from the daughters of Judea and of its princes, beautiful and wise, if he would send a general[1] leading a great army against Jerusalem, and would command that he be the king of Judea, and would take prisoner his uncle Hyrcanus, and kill Herod and his brother. The king agreed and sent him with a general leading a great army.

They marched into the land of Syria, and they killed a friend of Antony and some other Romans who were living there. From there, they marched against the sacred city, professing security and peace, and that Antigonus had only come to pray in the sanctuary, and then would return to his own friends. They entered the city, and after they were inside, they attacked and began to kill men, and to plunder the city, according to the orders of the king of Parthia. Herod and his men ran to defend the palace of Hyrcanus, but he sent his brother and commanded him to guard the road that leads from the walls to the palace. When he had occupied these positions, he picked some of his men and marched against the Parthians who were in the city. His brother followed with some of his own men, and they slaughtered the

CHAPTER 49

majority of the Parthians who were in the city, but the rest fled from the city.

When the Parthian general saw that things had not gone as planned, he despatched messengers to Herod and his brother, to negotiate for peace, informing them, that now he was satisfied with their valor and bravery, that they were preferable to Antigonus, and that for that reason he would order his army to help Hyrcanus, rather than Antigonus. His wish he confirmed by the most solemn oaths, so that Hyrcanus and Faisal believed him, but not Herod.

Hyrcanus and Faisal went out to the Parthian general and signified to him their reliance on him, and he advised them to go to his colleague who was in Damascus, and they went. When they arrived, he received them honorably, made a display of holding them in high esteem, and treated them courteously, although he had secretly given orders that they should be held as prisoners. Some of the main men of the land went to them, and told them of this plan, and advised them to flee and offered to help their escape, but they did not trust these men, thinking it was some plot against them, so they remained.

In the evening they were arrested. Faisal killed himself rather than be taken, but Hyrcanus was shackled in chains, and the Parthian general ordered that his ear be cut off,[2] so he might never be high priest again. Then he sent him to Iraq,[3] to the king of the Parthians.

When he arrived, the king ordered his chains to be removed and showed him kindness. He remained in Iraq as an honored guest until Herod demanded he be returned from the king of the Parthians. (When he was sent back to Herod, that which happened to him, happened to him.)

After this, the general traveled with Antigonus into the sacred city, and Herod was told what had been done to Hyrcanus and Faisal. Therefore, he sent his mother Cypris, his wife Marianne the daughter of Aristobulus, and her mother Alexandra, with horses and a great deal of baggage to Joseph his brother at Mount Seir, but he marched slowly with an army of a thousand men, waiting for the Parthians who might try to follow him. The Parthian general pursued him with his army, and Herod attacked them and defeated them, and they fled. After this, Antigonus' soldiers also pursued him and attacked him fiercely, and these he counter-attacked and slaughtered in great numbers. He then marched to the mountains of Seir and found his brother Josephus, who he ordered to secure the families in a safe place and to provide everything necessary for them. He gave them a great deal of money, so if needed, they might buy themselves provisions.

After leaving his men with his brother Josephus, he and a few companions went into Egypt, so he could take a ship to the land of the Romans. Cleopatra entertained him courteously and asked him to take command of her armies and the management of all her affairs. However, he said it was urgent for him to go to Rome. She gave him money and ships, and he traveled to Rome, resided with Antony, and told him what Antigonus had done, and what he had done to Hyrcanus and his brother, with the help of the Parthian king. Antony rode with him to Augustus and to the Senate and told them these things.

Chapter 49 Notes

1 While not named in this book, the Parthian general's name was recorded as Barzapharnes by Josephus.

2 Josephus reported it was Antigonus who cut off Hyrcanus' ear. It is unlikely that a Parthian general would have been familiar enough with the Torah to know this would prevent Hyrcanus from being a priest at the temple in Jerusalem. As the author must have had access to Josephus' writing, this appears to be an intentional alteration of the events. Combined with the removal of the name of the general, it suggests an intent to vilify the Parthians.

3 Arabic: ḥōrāk (حعراك)

The term found in the Arabic text appears to be an Arabic transliteration of hôråq (העיראק), meaning 'the Iraq' in Palestinian Aramaic, however, is not 'the Iraq' in Arabic, which is āl-ôrāq (العراق). It is unclear why an Arabic translator would render the name this way, but indicates the Arabic translator was living somewhere other than Iraq. The capital of the Parthian empire was moved to Ctesiphon (Κτησιφῶν), near modern Baghdad in 58 BC, and so the king was likely there in 40 BC when the events took place. The name 'Iraq' is accepted as having been used since at least the Persian era, as airga (𐎠𐎡𐎼𐎦), meaning 'lowlands,' and therefore, the term is rendered as 'Iraq,' in this translation.

Chapter 50

Augustus and the senate, once informed of what Antigonus had done, with unanimous consent appointed Herod king of Judea, commanding him to put a golden crown on his head, and to mount a horse, and that it could be proclaimed by trumpets preceding him, "Herod is king of Judea and the sacred city Jerusalem," which was done.

After, he rode back to Augustus. Augustus and Antony were at Antony's house, who had invited the senate and all the citizens of Rome to a banquet which he had prepared. They ate and drank, celebrated Herod joyously, and made a treaty, engraved in brass tablets, which were placed in the temples. They inscribed that day as the first of Herod's reign, and from that time it was taken for an era, by which years are counted.[1]

After this, Antony and Herod traveled by sea with a great army, and when they reached Antioch they divided their forces. Antony took a part and led it into the land of the Parthians which is Iraq and the parts adjacent. Herod commanded another part and went straight to Acre.

When Antigonus heard that Antony launched an expedition into the land of the Parthians and that Herod had reached Acre, he marched out from the sacred temple to the mountain Seir, to capture Josephus,

CHAPTER 50

Herod's brother, and those who were with him. He attacked them and besieged them, and cut off a canal by intercepting the water which flowed down to them. They were so dehydrated that they were all in dire straights, and Josephus debated fleeing. The families decided to surrender Antigonus if Josephus did flee, but God sent a great rainstorm to them that filled all their cisterns and vessels. Then their hearts were encouraged, and their condition was improved.

Josephus continued to repulse Antigonus[2] and his men from the fortress, and he could not gain any advantage over him. Herod marched quickly to Mount Seir, to return his brother and the families, and the men who were with him, to Jerusalem, where he found Antigonus besieging his brother. He launched a sudden attack on them, and Josephus and his men came out to help them, and the majority of Antigonus' army was destroyed, while he retreated to Jerusalem.

Herod pursued him with a great army of Judeans, who had joined him from every quarter when they heard he had returned. There were so many volunteers, that he did not need the Roman army. When Herod reached the sacred city, Antigonus locked the gates as he was approaching, and fought against him. He sent a lot of money to the commanders of the Roman army, asking them not to assist Herod, which they agreed to. Therefore, the war lasted a long time between Antigonus and Herod, with neither of them quickly defeating the other.

Chapter 50 Notes

1 This appears to be a reference to the Julian calendar, which was introduced by Julius Caesar in 45 BC. Herod became king in 37 BC, meaning that the calendar is off by 8 years. This is likely based on a calculation made shortly after 525 AD, as there was an 8-year gap in Greek, Latin, and Syriac Christian calendars when the calculations of Dionysius Exiguus were adopted.

Prior to 525, different Christian churches used the calculations of either Panodoros of Alexandria or Annianus of Alexandria to determine the Incarnation of Jesus. Both of these calculations were made circa 400 AD and differed by six months based on different interpretations of the Gospels. This was resolved in 525 when Dionysius Exiguus redid the calculations after it was decided that Jesus was not incarnated, and determined that the Annunciation of Jesus was 8 or 7.5 years earlier than previously accepted. The Orthodox Tewahedo churches continue to use a calendar that is 7.5 years off of the Julian calendar to denote the Incarnation of Jesus, based on the calculations of Annianus of Alexandria.

While this can be used to date the Palestinian Aramaic authorship to shortly after 525 AD, it also confirms that she was a Jew, as there would be no reason for a Christian to think that the Julian calendar of the Roman Empire was based on Herod becoming king of Judea.

2 Arabic: ȯntwny (أنطوني). Translation: Antony

This is universally considered a scribal error, as Antigonus was the leading the attack, not Antony, and therefore corrected in this translation. There is no evidence of Mark Antony leading an assault on Petra, where the siege is set.

Chapter 51

Thieves and those who envied the property of others had become common during the time of Antigonus. They lived in caves in the mountains where only one man could enter at a time. Secret places that few knew of, but were perfect for their needs. Even if someone found out they were there, they could not enter the caves, as a man was always present at the mouth who could easily repel anyone trying to enter.

Some of these men in the caves had amassed a large amount of arms, provisions, drink, and everything else they needed, both from the spoils that they had taken by attacking people and that which they had gained other ways, both legally and illegally.

When Herod learned of their activities, and found that the natural defenses were likely to slow down any approach, and also that men could not climb into the caves using ladders nor climb up any other way in secret, he used large wooden chests and filled them with men, (adding food and water,) with very long hooked spears. The chests he ordered to be lowered from the tops of the mountains the caves were in until they were outside the openings to the caves.

When they were outside the openings, he ordered that his men should attack in close combat with swords, and others below should attack and drag down the bodies with the hooked spears.

The chests were made, and filled with men, and some of them were let down. They reached the outside of the openings of the caves, without the people living there finding out. Then one of the men who were in the chests rushed into the caves, followed by his companions, and they killed the thieves who were in them, together with their followers and threw them down into the valleys below.

All the men that Herod sent copied these first, and in this exploit, their courage, bravery, and boldness was so conspicuous, that the like of it had never been seen before. They completely rooted out the robbers from all those parts.

Chapter 52

After leaving Herod, Antony marched from Antioch into the land of the Parthians and fought with the king of the Parthians, defeated him, killed him, conquered his country, and reduced the Parthians to submission to the Romans. Then he returned to this side of the Euphrates.

When his glory was reported to Herod, he decided to congratulate him on his victory and request he come meet with him in the holy land. He found a very large multitude amassed who wanted to approach Antony, which many Arabians opposed, preventing them from coming to Antony's presence. Herod marched against the Arabs, and slaughtered them, opening a passage for all who wished to approach Antony. This was reported to Antony before Herod arrived, and therefore he sent him a gold crown and a great many horses.

When Herod arrived, Antony received him courteously and praised him for his exploits against the Arabs. He attached to him Sosius a general of his army, with a large force, and ordered him to take him to the city of the sacred temple. He also gave him letters for all the country of Syria, which is from Damascus to the Euphrates, and from the Euphrates to the country of Armenia, saying to them, "Augustus, king of kings, and Antony his colleague, and the Roman senate, have now appointed Herod king over the Judeans, and they desire you to send out all your soldiers with Herod to assist him. If you act contrary to this, you must go to war with us." Then Antony marched to the sea coast, and from there into Egypt.

Herod and Sosius with his army commanded the forces of Syria, but when Herod approached Damascus, he found that his brother Josephus had left the sacred temple with an army of Romans, to besiege Jericho and cut down its crops. Against them came Pappus, a general of Antigonus' forces, who slaughtered thirty thousand of them, including Josephus Herod's brother, whose head was then cut off and given to Antigonus. Pheroras his other brother bought it for five hundred talents and buried it in the sepulchre of his fathers.

He heard also that Antigonus and Pappus were advancing against him with a large army. When Herod had determined exactly where they were, he decided to launch a preemptive strike on Antigonus and to crush him unexpectedly. He agreed with Sosius that he should take twelve thousand Romans and twenty thousand Judeans, and march rapidly against Antigonus, but that the others should slowly follow his footsteps with the remainder of the army.

Herod marched with his troops in formation and met Antigonus in the mountainous parts of Galilee, and they fought from midday until night. Then the armies separated, and Herod with some of his men spent the night in a certain house, but the house collapsed on them. They all escaped from the rubble with their lives, without a bone of any of them being broken.

Shortly afterward Herod rushed to fight Antigonus, and there was a great battle between them, but Antigonus fled into the sacred temple. Pappus continued to fight bravely, and the battle continued as he was high-spirited and very brave. The majority of Antigonus' army was killed on that day, including Pappus, whose head Pheroras cut off, and they took it to Herod, who ordered it to be buried.

When nothing remained of Antigonus' army, except prisoners and deserters, Herod ordered his men to rest and to eat and drink. He went to a certain bath which was in the next town and went into the bath unarmed. Hidden in the bath were three strong and brave men, holding drawn swords in their hands, who, when they saw him come into the bath unarmed, rushed out of the bath pushing each other out of the way, as they were afraid of him, and so he escaped.

After this, Sosius came, and they marched together to the city of the sacred temple, which they surrounded with a trench, and fierce battles took place between them and Antigonus. The majority of Sosius' men were killed, as Antigonus frequently defeated them, but he could not cause them to retreat due to their strength and endurance in facing his assaults. Then Herod defeated against Antigonus, and Antigonus fled, entered the city, and shut the gates against Herod, and Herod besieged him for a long time.

On a certain night, the guards at one of the gates fell asleep, which some of Herod's men discovered. Twenty of them ran with ladders and placed them against the wall, and then climbed up and killed the guards. Herod with his men rushed to the gate of the city which was near them and entered the city. After the Romans had captured it, they began to slaughter the citizens. At which point Herod, being concerned, asked Sosius, "If you destroy all my people, over whom will you appoint me as king?"

Sosius ordered the proclamation that the sword should be stayed, and no one was killed after the proclamation. However, Sosius' captains were eager for bounty and ran to plunder the temple of God. Herod met them at the gate, holding a drawn sword in his hand, and prevented them from entering. He sent to Sosius to restrain his men, promising them money, and Sosius ordered a proclamation to abstain from plunder, and they abstained.

CHAPTER 52

They searched for Antigonus and found him, and Antigonus was taken prisoner.

After these things, Sosius traveled into Egypt to his colleague Antony, taking with him Antigonus in chains. Herod sent Antony a glorious and magnificent gift: asking him to kill Antigonus, and Antony killed him.

This was in the third year of the reign of Herod, which also was the third year of Antigonus.

Chapter 53

When Herod was notified of the death of Antigonus, he considered himself secure that none of the royal Hasmonean family would contend with him. Therefore he spent his time elevating the dignity of, being kind to and promoting those who liked him and obeyed his will. He also worked to destroy those people, along with their families, who had aided those that opposed him, and in plundering their cattle and their other property.

He oppressed people, taking away their property, and pillaging all those who had escaped subjugation to the Judeans. He killed those who resisted him and plundered their goods. He also made an agreement with all who were obedient to him, that they should pay him money. He stationed guards at the gates of the sacred temple, who searched those who left, seized whatever gold or silver they found on anyone, and brought it to him. He also ordered the coffins of the dead to be searched, and whatever money any person might endeavor to carry out should also be taken. He piled up a tremendous mass of money like none of the kings of the second temple had amassed before.

Chapter 54

After the king of Parthia had set him free, Hyrcanus remained with the Iraqis,[1] in a most respectable position and with great honor. Herod was afraid something might induce the king of the Parthians to appoint him king and send him into the land of Judea. Therefore wishing to set his mind to peace, he concocted a scheme. He sent to the king of the Parthians a great gift, and a letter, in which he spoke of Hyrcanus' honors, and wanting to reward him. He mentioned how he had gone to Rome because of what Antigonus his brother's son had done to him, and now having attained the throne, with his affairs in order, he wanted to reward him properly for the benefits he had earned.

The king of the Parthians sent a messenger to Hyrcanus, saying, "If you wish to return into the land of Judea, return. However, I warn you to beware of Herod. I am clearly informing you that he does not seek good for you, but plans to render himself secure, as there is no one else he fears, except you. Therefore be very cautious of him, and do not be led into a trap."

The Judahites of Babylon also came to him and said similar words. They said to him, "You are now an old man, and not fit to be the high priest because of the injury that your nephew inflicted on you. Yet Herod is a bad man and a shedder of blood. He only recalls you because he is afraid of you. You do not lack anything among us, and you are with us in the position that you ought to be. Your family is in the best situation, so remain with us, and do not help your enemy against yourself."

But Hyrcanus would not accept their words, nor listen to the advice of anyone who advised him. He set out and journeyed to the sacred city, because of the great longing that he had for the temple of God, his family, and his country.

When he had approached the city, Herod met him, showing him so much honor and glory that Hyrcanus was deceived and trusted him. Herod in the public assembly, and before his own friends, called him 'Father' so he would not be seen as dishonorable by them, but never stopped plotting in his heart. Alexandra and Mariamne her daughter went to Hyrcanus and advised him to fear Herod, and counseled him to take care of himself, but he did not listen to them either. They repeated this to him again and again, advising him to flee to one of the kings of the Arabs, but he would not hear it until they eventually drove him to it with repeated warnings.

Then he wrote to the king of Nabataea,[2] and having sent for a man whose brothers Herod had killed, and then had confiscated his goods, and had exorcised many evils against him, he told him that he wanted to send with him a secret, swearing him to not tell it to anyone. He gave him money and the letter for the king of Nabataea and told him what he requested in the letter. The messenger after receiving the letter, thought that he would gain a high post with Herod, and would remove himself from the evil that he was constantly fearing from his hands if he told Herod about it, and this would be more profitable to him than keeping Hyrcanus' secret. In the other case, he was not safe, and not sure Herod would not hear about it eventually, so it would cause his destruction. He therefore took the letter to Herod and told him everything, who responded to him, "Carry the letter, as it is, to the king of the Nabataeans, and bring back his answer to me, so I may know it. Tell me also where are the men the king of the Nabataeans will send, so Hyrcanus may go back with them."

So the messenger went and carried Hyrcanus' letter to the king of the Nabataens, who rejoiced and sent some of his men, ordering them to go to a place near the sacred city and wait there until Hyrcanus came to them, and then to attend to Hyrcanus until they brought him into his presence. He also wrote this to Hyrcanus as an answer to his letter and sent it with the messenger. The men traveled with the messenger to the appointed place and waited there, but the messenger carried the letter to

Herod, who learned its contents. He also told him the place where the men were, and Herod sent people to arrest them.

Afterward, he sent for the Sanhedrin and also sent for Hyrcanus. When he arrived, he asked him, "Is there any exchange of letters between you and the king of the Nabateans?"

Hyrcanus answered, "No."

Then he asked him, "Did you send one so you might flee to him?"

He again answered, "No."

Herod ordered his messenger to come forward, and the Arabs, with their horses. He also brought out the replying letter, and it was read. Then he commanded Hyrcanus' head to be chopped off, and his head was chopped off, and no one dared speak a word for him.

Hyrcanus had saved Herod from a death which was justly awarded him in the assembly of judgment, commanding the assembly to be deferred until the morning, and sending away Herod that same night. However, he was destined to become his murderer regardless of his services to him and to his father. Hyrcanus was put to death when he was eighty years old, and he had reigned forty years. There was not one of the kings of the Hasmonaean family more praise-worthy in conduct, or more honorable in way of life.

Chapter 54 Notes

1 Arabic: ḥōrākyn (حعراكين)

The term found in the Arabic text appears to be a transliteration of hôrâqyn (העיראקין), meaning 'the Iraqis' in Palestinian Aramaic, however, is not 'the Iraqis' in Arabic, which is āl-ôrāqy (العراقي). Based on context, the original Aramaic text likely read "Hyrcanus remained in Iraqis," which is the translation used here. The Arabic translator appears to have been unclear about what the terms ḥōrāk and ḥōrākyn mean, treating them as the name of the capital city of the Parthians, however, at the time, that was Ctesiphon, in Iraq.

2 Arabic: ōrbyà (عَرَبِيّة). Translation: Arab woman (conceptually: Arabia)

The Arab king in question is accepted as being Malichus I (מנכו), who ruled Nabataea between 59 and 30 BC. As 'king of Arabia' is an imprecise translation, and 'king of Arab woman' would be a pointless translation, the name of his kingdom is used in this translation.

Chapter 55

Aristobulus the son of Hyreanus had a very beautiful body, exquisite figures, and intelligence that was unequalled. His sister Mariamne, the wife of Herod, was like him in beauty, and Herod was completely attached to her. Yet Herod was opposed to appointing Aristobulus as high priest in the place of his father, in case the Judeans, being loyal to him because of their loyalty to his father, should at some point in the future decide to make him the king. Therefore, he appointed one of the common priests who was not of the family of the Hasmonaeans to be the high priest.

This made Alexandra, the mother of Aristobulus angry, and she wrote to Cleopatra, requesting to have a letter from Antony sent to Herod, ordering him to remove the priest he had elevated and appoint her son Aristobulus as high priest instead. Cleopatra agreed to this, and asked Antony to write a letter to Herod about it and to send it by an important man from among his servants. Antony wrote a letter and sent it with his servant Gellius, and Gellius traveled to Herod and delivered Antony's letter to him. However, Herod rejected what Antony had ordered him to do, claiming that it was not customary among the Judeans to remove any priest from his position.

It happened that when Gellius saw Aristobulus, he became enamored with the beauty of his features and the perfection of his body. He would watch him, and one day he painted a picture of him, and sent it to Antony, writing beneath the picture that no man had fathered Aristobulus, but that an angel[1] had impregnated Alexandra. When the picture reached Antony, he was seized with a most earnest desire to see Aristobulus, and he wrote a letter to Herod, reminding him how he had appointed him king, and had assisted him against his enemies, reminding him of his kindnesses towards him. He also asked if he could send Aristobulus to him, and he threatened him regarding the words that he had sent back.

When Antony's letter was brought to Herod, he refused to send Aristobulus, knowing what Antony planned to do with him, and because of it, he refused to do it. He quickly removed the high priest he had appointed and established Aristobulus in his place.

Then he wrote to Antony, informing him that he had already done that which he had previously written to him about, and placed Aristobulus in his father's position before his most recent letter had arrived. He had delayed it initially because it was necessary to debate the matter with the priests and Judeans for many days as it was unusual, but it had happened according to his wish, he had immediately appointed him. However, now that he was appointed, it was not lawful for him to leave Jerusalem, as he was not king, but a priest in service of the temple. If he compelled him to leave, the Judeans would rebel and not allow him to leave even if he should kill the majority of them.

When Herod's letter reached Antony, he stopped asking for Aristobulus; and Aristobulus was made high priest. Then the feast of tabernacles came, and men assembled before the temple of God, and saw Aristobulus clothed in the sacerdotal robes standing at the altar. They heard him blessing them, and he pleased the men so much that they showed their affection for him in a very obvious way. When Herod was informed, he was very worried and feared that Aristobulus' supporters might gain strength, and he could demand the kingdom for him if he lived long enough. Therefore, he began to plot his death.

It was customary for the kings to go out, after the feast of Tabernacles, to some palatial estates in Jericho, which former kings had made. There were many gardens connecting them, in which there were wide and deep fish ponds, with streams of water flowing in and out. They had erected beautiful buildings in those gardens, and they also had built magnificent palaces in Jericho and handsome edifices.

(The author of the book claims that balsam plants grew commonly in Jericho, and that they were found nowhere else except there. That many kings had carried them from there into their own country, but none grew, except those which were carried into Egypt. That they did not die in Jericho until after the destruction of the second temple. Then they withered away, and never sprouted again.)[2]

So Herod went out to Jericho intent on pleasure, and Aristobulus followed him. When they arrived in Jericho, Herod commanded some of his servants to go down into the fish ponds, and play, as was customary. Also, if Aristobulus came down to them, they should play with him for some time, and then drown him. Herod sat in a banquet hall which he had prepared for himself, and Herod sent for Aristobulus and had him sit by his side. Additionally, the most important of his attendants and of his friends sat in his presence. He commanded food and drink to be brought, and ate and drank.

The attendants ran down to the water, as was the custom, and swam, and Aristobulus greatly wanted to go down with them to the water. When they were beginning to get drunk, he asked Herod for permission to join them, who answered, "This doesn't befit you, nor anyone like you."

When he was urgent, he admonished him and forbade him. When Aristobulus repeated his request to him, he answered him, "Do as you please."

Then Herod got up and went somewhere so he could take a nap, and Aristobulus went down to the water and played for a long time with the attendants, who, when they saw he was getting tired and wanted to leave, held him underwater, killed him, and pulled out his dead body.

There was a great uproar among the people; crying and wailing. Herod ran down to see what had happened, and when he saw Aristobulus dead he wailed and wept over him very tenderly with a great flood of tears. Then he ordered him to be carried to the sacred city, accompanied him to the city, and compelled the people to attend his funeral. There was no limit to the very highest honors that he did not offer him. He died when he was a youth of sixteen years of age, and his high priesthood lasted for only a few days.

Because of this, enmity grew between his mother Alexandra, and her daughter Mariamne, Herod's wife, and the mother and sister of Herod. The insults, and contempt that Mariamne showed them were well known, and although Herod knew about it, he did not forbid her or punish her because of his great love for her.

CHAPTER 55

He was also afraid that she might imagine that he loved the others, and so these things continued for a long time between these women. Herod's sister, who was endowed with the greatest malice, and intelligence for strategy, began to plot against Mariamne, but Mariamne was religious, upright, modest, and virtuous. She had little haughtiness, pride, or hatred towards her husband.

Chapter 55 Notes

1 Arabic: mlāk (مَلَاك). Translation: angel

The term is the South Levantine Arabic form of the word mlāk (مُلَّاك), which translates as 'angel' or 'divine messenger,' which does seem consistent with the implied meaning in the text. If the event is based on an actual event, it is likely that Gellius was referring to Mercury, the messenger of Jupiter, who was also described in Roman sources as a beautiful male youth. According to this book, Aristobulus was 16 at the time, and ephebophilia, the erotic interest in young adults aged 15 through 19 was common in certain ancient Greek and Roman cultures, so the story may be historically accurate. The fact that the author included the homosexual content, suggests she was female, as the Jewish culture became quite homophobic in the aftermath of the Persian and Greek dominions over Judea, and a male, regardless of sexual orientation would have probably omitted any homosexual content. As the author does appear to have intended this verse to read that an 'angel' fathered Aristobulus, that is the translation used here.

2 This scribal note is a reference to what is known in English as the 'Balm of Gilead,' based on William Tyndale's translation of the Old Testament in the early 1500s. Historically, it was known as Balsam of Matariyya in medieval alchemical texts. Based on Classical era works, the balm was used since at least 287 BC, and was also called the 'balm of Egypt,' or 'balm of Mecca.' Many Classical era historians referred to the balsam as being indigenous to Jericho, however, Diodorus Siculus deviated from this in his 40-volume *Bibliotheca Historica* which was published

between 60 and 30 BC, claiming it also grew in Arabia. In 79 AD, Josephus claimed the balsam shrubs were a gift from the Queen of Sheba to Solomon, circa 950 BC, meaning they originated in Yemen or Eritrea.

The earliest clear record of them was in Theophrastus' 10-volume *Historia Plantarum*, published between 350 and 287 BC, in which he described them as only growing on two groves in Jericho, the larger being 20 acres in size. Pompey had brought one to Rome after his conquest of Judea in 65 BC, however, it appears to have died quickly. Emperor Vespasian did the same thing in 79 AD, after the First Jewish-Roman War, although it again does not appear to have survived long. This seems to be confirmed by the writing of Tacitus, circa 100 AD, which claims that the only thing that grew in Judea that did not also grow in Italy was this balsam shrub. In 81 AD, Emperor Titus occupied and then nationalized the balsam groves in Jericho after Judean nationalists attempted to destroy the groves. After this, they were under public administration. According to the Roman physician Galen of Pergamon, by the mid 2nd century AD, it grew all over Palestine.

According to Pedanius Dioscorides 5-volume *De Materia Medica*, published between 50 and 70 AD, the resin from this shrub was used for many diverse things, including epilepsy, gripes, sciatica, vertigo, and respiratory problems like coughing, asthma, pleurisy, and pneumonia, as well as menstrual issues, and could be used as an abortifacient. In medieval alchemical literature, it became a mythical 'cure-all' drug, although the groves in Judea appear to have been destroyed at some point. This likely happened in the early Byzantine era, when most other plants that could be used to make abortifacient agents were destroyed, which suggests the author lived after the 5th century AD.

Chapter 56

Cleopatra, the queen of Egypt, was the wife of Antony, and she discovered methods of adorning and painting herself through which women allure men, as no other woman in the world had ever found.

So much so, that while she was an older woman, she seemed like a little unmarried girl, and even more delicate and more fair. Antony also found in her those methods of beauty and those means of creating pleasure which he had never found in the great many women he had enjoyed. She so completely gained possession of Antony's heart, that no room was left in it for affection to any other person. She was able to persuade him to remove kings who were subject to the Romans, for her own private considerations, and he obeyed her, putting to death kings at her request. Some he left alive by her orders, making them her servants or slaves.

This was told to Augustus, who wrote to him, condemning such conduct, and ordering him not to do this again. Antony told Cleopatra what Augustus had written to him, and she told him to revolt from Augustus and convinced him that it would be very easy.

He agreed with her opinion, and openly betrayed Augustus, gathering an army and supplies, so he might travel by sea to Antioch, and from there march by land to meet Augustus wherever he might find him. He also sent for Herod, so he could accompany him. Herod traveled with a powerful army and extensive supplies. When he had arrived, Antony said to him, "Reason advises us to make an expedition against the Arabs, and to attack them, for we are not secure, and they may launch an invasion of Judea and the land of Egypt, as soon as we have turned our backs."

Antony departed by sea, and Herod marched towards the Arabs. Cleopatra sent a general named Athenio with a great army, to assist Herod in subduing the Arabs, and she commanded him to place Herod and his men in the first rank and to make an agreement with the king of the Arabs, that they together should surround Herod and cut his men to pieces. She desired this in hopes of obtaining possession of everything Herod was worth. Alexandra also previously asked her to induce Antony to execute Herod, which indeed she had done, but Antony refused to commit this act.

Her motivation was also caused by the fact that Cleopatra had once longed for Herod, and had desired intercourse with him, but he restrained himself, for he was chaste. These were the causes that had led her to this line of action.

Athenio came to Herod according to the command of Cleopatra and sent a messenger to make an agreement with the king of the Arabs, so he might surround him. When Herod and the Arabs met and engaged, Athenio and his men attacked Herod, who was caught between the two armies, and the battle grew fierce against him both in front and behind. Herod understood what had happened, collected his men, and fought vigorously until they were beyond the reach of both armies. After great exertion, he returned to the holy temple.

Then a great earthquake happened in the land of Judea, which had not occurred since the time of Jeroboam II[1] based on the number of men and animals that were destroyed. This alarmed Herod a great deal, caused him tremendous fear, and broke down his spirit. He took counsel with the Sanhedrin of Judea about making agreements with all nations around them, intending peace and tranquillity, and the end of wars and bloodshed. He also sent ambassadors regarding these matters to the surrounding nations, all of whom embraced the peace to which he had invited them, except the king of the Arabs, who ordered the ambassadors Herod had sent to be put to death. He thought that Herod had done this because his men had been destroyed in the earthquake, and therefore, being weakened, he had turned to making peace. Therefore he decided to go to war with Herod, and so he amassed a large and well-provisioned army, and he marched against him.

CHAPTER 56

When this was told to Herod, he was very angry for two reasons: one, because of his ambassadors being killed, an act which none of the kings had before committed, and two, because he had dared to attack him, imagining in his mind his weakness and lack of troops. He wished to show him that the matter was otherwise, so all that he'd sent ambassadors to requesting peace might know that he did not do this through any fear or weakness, but from a wish that was kind and good, so no one would dare make attempts against the Judeans, or imagine in his mind that they were weak. He also wished to take vengeance on the king of the Arabs for his ambassadors, so he decided to rapidly march against him.

Therefore he amassed his troops from the land of Judea, and said to them, "You are aware of the killing of our ambassadors perpetrated by the Arab, an act which no king before has committed. He thinks that we have been weakened and have become powerless. He has dared to provoke us and thinks that he will obtain all his desires over us, and he will never stop eternal warfare against us. Therefore, you must struggle against difficulties, so you may show your bravery, subdue your enemies, and carry off their plunder. Although fortune may at one time show herself favorable, at another time she is against us, as is normal and usual in the rapidly shifting fortune of this world. In truth, you must immediately undertake an expedition to take vengeance on those oppressors and to curb the audacity of all who hold you in contempt. If you say, 'This earthquake has disheartened us, and has destroyed great numbers of us,' you know full well, that it has destroyed none of the fighting men, but only others. We should not find it unreasonable to think that it has destroyed the worst among our people, and has left the best to survive. It is also not in doubt, that this has improved your spirits and your inward feelings.

But the duty of he whom God has saved from destruction, and has preserved from ruin, requires that he should obey Him, and should do what is good and right. Truly no obedience is more honorable or glorious, than to seek retribution for the oppressed from the oppressor, and to subdue the enemies of God and his religion and people, by aiding those who show obedience and attention to Him. You know what recently happened between us and the Arabs, when they surrounded us with Athenio, and how the great and good God helped us against them, and saved us from them. Fear God, following your ancient custom, and the praiseworthy custom of your forefathers. Prepare yourselves against this enemy before he makes ready against you, and be beforehand with him before he anticipates you: and God will supply you with aid and succor against your enemy."

When the men had heard Herod's speech, they replied that they were ready to undertake the expedition, and would leave without delay. He thanked God, and thanked them, and ordered many sacrifices to be offered. He also ordered an army to be raised, and a great multitude was gathered from the tribes of Judah and Benjamin.

Herod marched against the king of the Arabs and engaged him, and the battle grew fierce between them, five thousand Arabs were killed. Then there was a second battle where four thousand Arabs were killed, therefore, the Arabians returned to their camp and remained there. Herod could do nothing against them, as the place was fortified, but he remained with his army, besieging them in that place, and not allowing them to leave. They remained five days in this state, and a most horrific thirst came over them. They sent ambassadors to Herod with a most valuable tribute, asking for a truce, and freedom to draw water for drinking, but he would not hear them and continued the same furious hostility.

The Arabs then said, "Let us go out against these people, as it is better for us to conquer or die than to die of dehydration." And they went out against them, and

Herod's forces defeated them, and slaughtered nine thousand of them. Herod with his men pursued the Arabs as they fled, killing great numbers of them, and he besieged their cities and captured them. They begged for their lives, promising obedience, to which he agreed and then left them, and returned into the sacred temple.

(The Arabs mentioned in this book are the Arabs who lived from the country of Seir as far as the Hejaz and the adjacent regions, and they were renowned and great in numbers.)

Chapter 56 Notes

1 Arabic: hrbôā (هربعا)

Based on context, the king in question has to have been King Jeroboam II (יָרָבְעָם), who ruled over Judah during the great earthquake of circa 760 BC. The strange Arabic stelling is likely derived from the Greek spelling of Hieroboam (Ἱεροβοάμ), via a lost intermediate form in another language. The earthquake of circa 760 BC is estimated to have been between 7.8 and 8.2 on the Richter scale, while the earthquake of 31 BC was an estimated 7 on the Richter scale. According to Josephus, 30,000 Judeans died in the earthquake of 31 BC.

Chapter 57

When Antony had marched out of Egypt into the country of the Romans, and had engaged Augustus, terrible battles took place between them, in which victory sided with Augustus, and Antony fell in battle. Augustus captured his camp and all that was in it. After this was done, he proceeded to Rhodes, intending to take ships from there to Egypt.

Reports were brought to Herod, and he was very concerned when he heard Antony was dead. He greatly feared Augustus, and he decided to go to him, to salute him and congratulate him. Therefore he sent his mother and sister with his brother, to a fortress he had in Mount Seir. He sent also his wife Mariamne and her mother Alexandra to Alexandrium, under the care of Josephus a Tyrian, ordering him to kill his wife and her mother immediately if he heard a report of his death. Then he traveled to Augustus with a very valuable tribute.

Augustus had already decided to put Herod to death because he had been a friend and supporter of Antony, and because he had previously agreed to march with Antony to attack him. Therefore, when Augustus was informed of the arrival of Herod, he ordered him into his presence, allowing him to wear his royal habit, but not his crown, which he had ordered to be removed from his head.

When he was in his presence, having removed his crown as Augustus had commanded, he said, "Oh king, is it because of my love of Antony you have been so enraged with me that you have taken the crown from my head, or was it because of some other reason? If you are angry with me because of my obedience to Antony, honestly, I admit, I followed him because he treated me well, and placed the crown upon my head which you have taken off. Indeed, he did request my assistance against you, which I gave him, as he also helped me many times, but I was not present at the battle where he fought you, nor have I drawn my sword against you, nor fought you. Instead, I was engaged in subduing the Arabs. I never failed to supply him with men, arms, and provisions, as his friendship and his good deeds required of me. In all honesty, I am sorry that I left him, because now men may think I deserted my friend when he needed my help."

"Certainly, if I had been with him, I would have helped him with all my strength and would have encouraged him if he had been afraid, and would have strengthened him if he had been weakened, and would have lifted him up if he had fallen until God should have ruled matters as He pleased. This truly would have been less terrible for me, than that it should be thought that I had failed a man who had asked my aid, and therefore it is thought that my friendship is of little value. In my opinion, he fell through his own stupidity, in yielding to that enchantress Cleopatra. I had advised him to kill her, and so to remove her spell over him, but he did not agree. But now, if you have removed the crown from my head, certainly you will not remove from me my wisdom and my courage, and whatever I am, I will be a friend to my friends and an enemy to my enemies."

Augustus replied to him, "Antony we have indeed conquered with our troops, but you, we will master by converting you to us, and will take care, by our good offices towards you, that your affection to us shall be doubled, because you are worthy of this. Antony committed treason because of the advice of Cleopatra. She is also the reason he behaved ungratefully towards us, returning for our kindnesses with evils, and for our favours with rebellion. However, we are glad of the war which you have waged with the Arabs, who are our enemies. Whoever is your enemy, is ours also, and whoever is subservient to you, is also to us."

Then Augustus ordered the golden crown to be placed back on Herod's head, and as many provinces to be added to him as he already had. Herod accompanied Augustus into Egypt, and all the things which Antony had destined for Cleopatra transpired. Then Augustus departed to Rome, but Herod returned to the sacred city.

Chapter 58

Josephus, the husband of Herod's sister, had told Mariamne that Herod had ordered him to put her and her mother to death, as soon as he himself died when visiting Augustus. She already had a dislike of Herod, since the time when he killed her father and brother, and to this a great deal more hatred was added when she heard of the orders that he had given against her.

Therefore, when Herod returned from Egypt, he found her completely overwhelmed by her hatred of him. This greatly troubled him, he tried to reconcile with her by all possible methods. But his sister came on a certain day, after some arguments had taken place between her and Mariamne, and said to him, "Certainly Joseph my husband has been fornicating with Mariamne."

Herod paid no attention to her words, knowing how pure and chaste Mariamne was. After this, Herod went to see Mariamne that night, and behaved kindly and affectionately towards her, musing on his love for her, saying everything he could think of, to which she replied, "Did you ever see a man love another, and order him to be put to death? Would he not hate him, if shown proof of this?"

Then Herod realized that Josephus had revealed to Mariamne the secret he had entrusted to him. He had believed that he would not have done that unless she had given herself to him, and he believed what his sister had told him. He immediately departed from Mariamne, as he loathed and despised her.

When his sister heard of this, she went to the cupbearer, gave him money and some poison, and said, "Take this to the king, and say to him, 'Mariamne the king's wife gave me this poison and this money, ordering he to mix it into the king's drink.'"

The cupbearer did this, and when the king saw the poison, did not doubt the truth of it. He immediately gave orders to behead Josephus his brother-in-law, and also ordered Mariamne to be put in chains, until the Sanhedrin could be present, and could pass sentence upon her. Herod's sister was afraid that what she had done would be found out, and she would be executed and Mariamne set free, so she said to him, "My king if you delay Mariamne's death until tomorrow, you will not be able to do it. As soon as it becomes known that you seek her execution, the whole house of her father will come, and all their servants and neighbors, and will interfere; and you will not be able to obtain a warrant for her execution until after great riots."

Herod replied, "Do as it seems best to you."

Herod's sister sent quickly for a man to bring Mariamne out to the place of execution, and send her woman servants and other women to insult her and berate her with all kinds of indecent claims, but she said nothing back to any of them, nor even glance in their direction. She did not blush from this treatment, nor allow any fear or confusion to appear in her, and her gait was not altered. With her dignified manner, she proceeded to the place where she was led to be executed, knelt down, and held out her neck voluntarily. She departed this life renowned for religion and chastity, marked by no crime, and branded with no guilt. She was not completely free from haughtiness, due to the habits of her family. This was not the least cause of Herod's attention and affection towards her, because of her elegance, and therefore, she suspected no change in him towards her.

Herod had begotten two sons through her namely, Alexander and Aristobulus, who, when their mother was executed, were living in Rome. He had sent them there, to learn the literature and language of the Romans. Afterward, Herod repented that he had killed his wife, and he was so affected by grief from his actions in her death, that he contracted a disease that almost killed him. After Mariamne was dead, her mother Alexandra began scheming to kill Herod. He found out and killed her as well.

Chapter 59

When reports reached Alexander and Aristobulus of the murder of their mother by Herod, they were overcome by grief. They departed Rome and traveled to the sacred city, paying no respect to their father Herod as they had formerly done. They felt hatred for him in their minds because of their mother's death.

Alexander had married the daughter of King Archelaus,[1] and Aristobulus had married the daughter of Herod's sister. When Herod saw that they paid him no respect, he realized that they hated him, and he avoided them. This did not escape the attention of the young men and the rest of his family.

King Herod had married a wife before Mariamne named Dosithea through which he had a son named Antipater. Therefore, when Herod saw his two sons disrespecting him, as mentioned above, he brought his wife Dosithea to his palace and attached to himself his son Antipater, committing to him all his affairs, and he appointed him by will his successor.

Antipater persecuted his brothers Alexander and Aristobulus, intending to procure peace for himself while his father lived so that after his death he might have no rival. Therefore, he said to his father, "In truth, my brothers are seeking an inheritance because of the family of their mother, because it is more noble than the family of my mother. Therefore, they have a better claim than I have to the fortune that the king has judged me worthy of. Because of this, they are working to put you to death, and they will kill me soon after."

He frequently repeated this to Herod, also secretly sending to him persons to insinuate this to him, which might induce in him a greater hatred towards them.

In the interim Herod traveled to Rome to Augustus, taking with him his son Alexander. When he had arrived in Augustus' presence, Herod complained to him of his son, requesting that he would punish him. But Alexander said, "Indeed, I do not deny my anguish on account of the murder of my mother for no reason. Even wild animals show affection to their mothers better than men and love them more. However, I completely deny that I am planning to kill him, and I clear myself of it before God. I am possessed of the same feelings toward my father as toward my mother. I am not the sort of man to bring upon myself the guilt of a crime towards my parents, and more especially eternal torments."

Alexander wept bitterly and wailed loudly, and Augustus pitied him, and all the chiefs of the Romans, who were standing nearby also wept and cried. Then Augustus asked Herod to take back his sons into his former kindness and intimacy, and he asked Alexander to kiss his father's feet, which he did. He also ordered Herod to embrace and kiss him, and Herod obeyed him.

Afterward, Augustus ordered a magnificent gift for Herod, and it was brought to him. After passing some days with him, Herod returned to the sacred temple, summoned the Sanhedrin of Judea, and said, "You know that Antipater is my eldest son and firstborn, but his mother is not from a noble family. The mother of my sons Alexander and Aristobulus is of the family of the high priests and kings. Moreover, God has enlarged my kingdom and has extended my power. Therefore it seems good to me to appoint my three sons to equal authority so that Antipater shall have no command over his brothers, nor shall his brothers have command over him. Therefore, obey all three, you assembly of men. Don't interfere in anything that their minds may agree on. Don't propose anything which may produce confusion and disagreement among them. Do not drink with them, nor talk too much with them. As from that, it will happen that one of them may unguardedly state to you his plans against his brother, which you may use to manipulate them. You will follow your agreements with one of them, according to what seems good to him, and you will bring them to destruction, and you yourselves will also be destroyed. It is your lot, my sons, to be obedient to God, and to me, so you may live long, and that your affairs may prosper."

Soon afterward he embraced and kissed them, and commanded the people to leave.

However, what Herod wanted did not happen, as the hearts of his sons were not united in agreement. Antipater wanted everything to be put into his hands, as his father had formerly ordered. For his brothers, it did not seem fair that he should be viewed as equal to them. Antipater was endowed with perseverance, cunning, and the art of deceptive friendships, but not his two brothers. Antipater sent spies to observe his brothers, who would bring him reports about them. He also planted others who would carry false reports of them to Herod.[2] Yet when Antipater was in the presence of the king and heard anyone stating such things about his brothers, he rejected the charge they made, claiming that the authors were uncreditable, and asking the king not to believe the reports. Antipater did this, so he might not inspire any doubt or suspicion in the king regarding his own involvement. From this, the king had no doubt that he was well-inclined towards his brothers and wished them no harm.

When Antipater realized this, he used his uncle Pheroras for his purpose, and his aunt, as these were at enmity with his brothers regarding their mother's fate. He offered Pheroras a valuable gift, requesting him to tell the king that Alexander and Aristobulus had made a plan to murder the king. Herod was well inclined towards Pheroras his brother, and listened to whatever he said, as he paid to him a large sum out of the provinces he governed on the bank of the Euphrates. Pheroras did as he requested, and afterward, Antipater went to Herod, and said to him, "My king, in truth my brothers have hatched a plot to destroy me."

Antipater also gave money to the king's three eunuchs, so they should say, "Alexander has given us money, so he may wickedly use us to kill you, but when we refused it, he threatened to kill us."

The king was angry with Alexander and ordered him to be chained, and he arrested and tortured all of Alexander's servants until they confessed what they knew about Alexander's plot to murder him. Many of these, though they died being tortured, never told a lie about Alexander, but some of them, being unable to endure the painful torment, concocted lies as a way of freeing themselves, claiming that Alexander and Aristobulus had planned to attack the king, and kill him, and then flee to Rome. Then they would receive an army from Augustus to march against the sacred temple, kill their brother Antipater, and seize the throne of Judea.

CHAPTER 59

The king commanded Aristobulus to be arrested and put in chains, and he was shackled and placed with his brother.

When news of Alexander was brought to his father-in-law Archelaus, he went to Herod, pretending to be furious with Alexander, as if, on hearing a report of the intended parricide, he had come on purpose to see whether his daughter, the wife of Alexander, was aware of the plot, and had not revealed it to him, so he might put her to death. However, if she was not aware of anything of the kind, he might divorce her from Alexander, and take her home.

Archelaus was a prudent, wise, and eloquent man, and when Herod had heard his words, and was satisfied with his prudence and honesty, he decided he liked him, and he trusted him, and relied on him without the slightest hesitation. Archelaus therefore, discovering Herod's inclination towards him, after a long friendship, said to him one day when they had retired together, "Truly, king, while considering your affairs I have found that you, now being advanced in years want peace of mind, and to have solace in your sons. However, you have received the opposite from them, grief and anxiety. Moreover, I have considered regarding your two sons, and I do not think you have been incorrect in deserving them to treat you well. You have promoted them and made them kings, and have left nothing which might drive them to plot your death, nor have they any cause for considering this business. Perhaps this has come from some malicious person, who desires evil against you and them, or who through envy or enmity has induced you to hate them."

"If therefore he has gained influence over you, who is an old man, endowed with knowledge, information, and experience, changing you from paternal mildness to cruelty and fury against your children how much easier could he have provoked them, who are young, inexperienced, and unguarded, and with no knowledge of men and their guile, so that he has gained from them that which he wished in this matter. Consider therefore your affairs, king, and do not listen to the words of informers, nor do anything quickly against your children. Inquire who has been plotting evil against you and them."

The king replied to him, "Indeed the thing is as you have stated. I wish that I knew who has induced them to do this."

Archelaus answered, "It is your brother Pheroras."

The king replied, "It might be."

After this, the king changed his behavior towards Pheroras. When Pheroras realized it, he became afraid of him. He went to Archelaus, and said to him, "I see that the king is changed towards me, therefore I ask you to reconcile his mind to me, removing the feelings which he has in his heart against me."

Archelaus replied to him, "I will do it if you will promise to tell the king the truth regarding the plots which you have made against Alexander and Aristobulus," and he agreed to this.

After a few days, Archelaus said to the king, "Oh king, a man's relatives are to him like his own limbs, and as it is good for a man if any one of his limbs becomes affected by some disease which infects it, to restore it by medicines, even although it may cause him pain. It is not good to cut it off, or the pain could increase, the body becomes weakened, and the limbs should fail. From the loss of that limb, he would be very inconvenienced, but if he endures the pains of the medical treatment, the limb may become better, and may be healed, and his body may return to its former perfectness and strength. It is like this for a man, whenever any of his relatives changes towards him, from any abominable cause whatever, it is preferable to reconcile him back to himself, alluring him to civility and friendship, admitting his excuses, and dismissing the charges against him. It is preferable that he does not put him to death quickly, nor send him too far away from him. The relatives of a man are his supporters and assistants, and his honor and praise are found through them. Through them, he obtains that which he could not obtain. Pheroras truly is the king's brother, and the son of his father and of his mother. He confesses his fault, begging the king to spare him, and to forget his error."

The king replied, "I will do this," and he ordered Pheroras to come before him.

When he was in the king's presence, he said to him, "I have sinned now in the sight of the great and good God, and the king, devising schemes and plans which might injure the affairs of the king and his sons, and by my lies. That which made me act like this was that the king took a certain woman away from me, my concubine, and separated her from me."

The king said to Archelaus, "I have pardoned Pheroras, as you requested me, and I find that you have cured the disease which was in our affairs through your soothing methods, even as an ingenious physician heals the corruptions of a sick body. Therefore I ask you to pardon Alexander and reunite your daughter with her husband, as I view her as my daughter. I know that she is wiser than he is and that she guides him away from many things through her wisdom and her advice. Therefore, I beg you, do not separate them and destroy him, as he agrees with her, and obtains many advantages from her guidance."

Archelaus answered, "My daughter is the king's servant, but my mind has detested him lately, because of his evil plans. Therefore, let the king permit me to divorce him from my daughter, and the king may unite her to whichever of his servants he pleases."

The king replied, "Do not reject my request. Let your daughter remain with him, and do not argue with me."

Archelaus stated, "Surely I will do it, and will not argue with the king in anything that he shall ask of me."

Soon afterward, Herod ordered Alexander and Aristobulus to be released from their chains and to come before him. When they were in his presence, they prostrated themselves before him and confessed their faults, excusing themselves, and begging for pardon and forgiveness. He commanded them to stand up and told them to approach him. He kissed them and ordered them to go to their own homes and to return the next day.

They came to eat and drink with him, and he reinstated them in a place of greater honor. He gave Archelaus seventy talents, and a golden couch, ordering all the prominent men among his friends to offer valuable gifts to Archelaus, and they did so. After this, Archelaus left the city of the sacred temple and returned to his own country. Herod accompanied him, and after some time, left him and returned to the sacred temple.

Nevertheless, Antipater did not abandon his plots against his brothers, so he might make them repulsive. It happened that a certain man came to Herod, having some valuable and handsome articles, with which kings are usually won, and these he presented to the king, who, taking them from him, repaid him for them. The man obtained a very high place in his affections, and having been added to his retinue, enjoyed his confidence. This man was named Eurycles. When Antipater saw that this man had completely gained his father's favor, he offered him money, asking he would carefully insinuate to Herod that his two sons Alexander and Aristobulus were planning to murder him, which the man promised to do. Soon afterwards he went to Alexander, and became friendly and familiar with him to the degree that he was known to be his friend, and it was made known to the king that he was close with him.

After this, he went aside with the king, and said to him, "Certainly you have this right over me, king, that nothing ought to prevent me from giving you good advice. In truth, I have a matter which the king ought to know, and which I ought to tell to you."

The king asked him, "What have you heard?"

CHAPTER 59

The man answered him, "I heard Alexander saying, 'Truly God has deferred vengeance on my father for the death of my mother, of my grandfather, and of my relatives without any crime, that it may take place by my hand. I hope that I shall take vengeance for them upon him.' He has agreed with some elders to attack you, and he wished to include me in the plans that he has formulated, but I consider it a crime because of the king's acts of kindness towards me, and his liberality. My intention is to admonish him well, and to report this to him, for he has both eyes and understanding."

When the king had heard these words, he could not dismiss them, but quickly began to make inquiries as to their truth. He found out nothing that he could rely on, except a letter forged in the name of Alexander and Aristobulus to the governor of a certain town, which read:

> We want to kill our father and flee to you. Therefore prepare us a place where we may remain until the people amass around us, and our affairs are settled.

This was confirmed to the king and appeared probable, so he seized the governor of that city and tortured him so he might confess what was written in the letter. This man denied it, clearing himself from the charge, nor was anything proved against them in this matter, or in anything else which the informer had charged. Herod ordered them to be seized and bound with chains and shackles anyway. Then he went to Tyre, and from Tyre to Caesarea, taking them with him in chains. All the captains and all the soldiers pitied them, but no one interceded for them with the king, or else he would implicate himself in what the informer had claimed.

There was an old warrior in the army who had a son in the service of Alexander. When the old man saw the terrible condition of Herod's two sons, he pitied their change of fortune, and cried out with as loud a voice as he could, "Pity is gone! Goodness and piety have vanished away! Truth has left the world!"

Then he said to the king, "You are merciless to your children, an enemy to your friends, and a friend to your enemies! You listen to the words of informers and of persons who wish no good towards you!"

The enemies of Alexander and Aristohulus ran up to him, and reproved him, saying to the king, "King, it is not love towards you and towards your sons that made this man say this. He simply wants to shout out the hatred which he carries in his heart towards you and to speak ill of your counsel and administration, as being a faithful adviser. Some observers have informed us of him, that he had already made an agreement with the king's barber, to kill him with a razor while he was shaving him."

The king ordered that the old man, his son, and the barber be arrested, and the old man and the barber to be caned until they should confess. They were brutally beaten with canes and were subjected to various kinds of torture but they confessed nothing of what they had not done.

When the son of the old man saw the sad condition of his father and the state to which he had come, he pitied him and thought that he would be freed if he himself confessed that which was accused of his father, if he received a promise for his life from the king. Therefore he said to the king, "My king, give me security for my father and myself, so I can tell you what you are asking about."

The king said, "You may have this."

To which he replied, "Alexander made an agreement with my father that he should kill you, and my father made an agreement with the barber, as has been told you."

Then the king commanded that old man and his son to be executed, along with the barber. He also ordered both his sons Alexander and Aristobulus to be taken to Sebastia,[3] and there to be executed by being hung on a gibbet, and they were taken there and killed by being hung on a gibbet.

Alexander had two sons who survived him, namely, Tigranes and Alexander, through the daughter of King Archelaus, and Aristobulus left three sons, namely, Aristobulus, Agrippa, and Herod. But the history of Herod's son Antipater has already been described in our former writing.

Chapter 59 Notes

1 Arabic: ȯrḫylāws (أرخيلاوس). Translation: Archelaus

King Archelaus (Ἀρχέλαος) ruled Cappadocia between 36 BC and 17 AD. His family experienced a similar chain of events as the Hasmonean and Herodian dynasties. His grandfather, also known as Archelaus, was the first high priest and Roman client ruler of the region around Comana, in Cappadocia, in modern central Turkey. In 47 BC, Julius Caesar deposed Archelaus' father, also called Archelaus, from the priesthood and replaced him as ruler of Comana, as he had supported Pompey. In 36 BC, Achelaus' mother, who was a courtisan, seduced Mark Antony and convinced him to execute King Ariarathes X of Cappadocia and install her son as king. He is reported to have married his daughter Glaphyra to Prince Alexander of Judea in 17 or 18 BC. Like Herod, Archelus was despised by the people he ruled.

2 Arabic: bylāts (بيلاطس). Translation: Pilate

It is unclear who this is, and it is generally accepted as a scribal error. The Roman Prefect of Judea named Pontus Pilate (Pontius Pilatus) was not appointed to the position until decades later. The majority opinion is that he ruled Judea between 27 and 37 BC, although some scholars have argued for an earlier date, beginning in 17 through 19 AD. The events in this verse happened in approximately 10 BC. It is unlikely Pontius Pilate would have been present, however, another Roman named Pilate may have been, nevertheless, the next sentence indicates this is a reference to the king, who was Herod. The error suggests the Arabic translator was a Christian, as Pilate was not that significant in Judaism.

3 Arabic: sbstyà (سبسطية). Translation: Sebastia

Herod renamed the ancient village the Samaritans called Šōmrōn (ܫܘܡܪܘܢ) to Sebasti (Σεβαστη / סבסטיה) in honor of emperor Augustus.

Also Available

ALSO AVAILABLE

- Octateuch: The Original Orit

ENOCH AND METATRON SERIES:
- Books of Enoch Collection

- Books of Enoch and Metatron Collection

- Books of Metatron Collection

- Secrets of Enoch

OTHER TRANSLATIONS:
- Apocalypses of Ezra

- Arabic Maccabees

- Life of Adam and Eve

- Memories of the New Kingdom

- Septuagint's Esther and the Vetus Latina Esther

- Septuagint's Ezekiel and the Ba'al Cycle

- Septuagint's Job and the Testament of Job

- Septuagint's Proverbs and the Wisdom of Amenemope

- The Amarna Letters

- Testaments of the Patriarchs Collection

- Tobit and Ahikar

- Ugaritic Texts: Ba'al Cycle

- Wisdom of Ahikar

www.ingramcontent.com/pod-product-compliance
Lightning Source LLC
Chambersburg PA
CBHW061140120626
46546CB00005B/1862